THE COMPLETE JAPANESE

COOKBOOK

140 Easy Recipes For Cooking At Home Tasty Asian Food

Maki Blanc

JAPANESE

COOKBOOK

70 Easy Recipes For
Traditional Food From Japan

Maki Blanc

The trademarks that are used are without any consent, and the publication of the trademark is without permission or backing by the trademark owner. All trademarks and brands within this book are for clarifying purposes only and are the owned by the owners themselves, not affiliated with this document.

Contents

Introduction

While Japan is a small world, each area and even town has its distinct flavor. Food from the Kanto areas (the eastern part of the big island) and the Kansai area (the western part of the big island) are the most popular. Kanto cuisine is known for its bold flavors, while Kansai cuisine is known for its soft seasoning. Many dishes in the Kansai and Kanto areas are prepared differently. Traditional Japanese meals involve a cup of fried rice, which can be eaten for breakfast, noon, or supper. Okazu is the side item that is eaten with grain and soup. Rice is a favorite of Japanese cuisine. Rice cakes are also very popular. They come in various flavors and can be prepared in various ways, including boiling and grilling.

With an endless range of ethnic and seasonal foods, Japanese cuisine promises an array of culinary delights. Remote food vendors to centuries-old ryotei, scenic dining spots, and seasonal changes built cottages over rivers, inexpensive chain shops, and exclusive theme cafes about samurai and robots can all be found in Japan's restaurants. Many places specialize in one kind of dish, while others serve a wide range of options.

Perfect arrangement, pure flavors, and specialty foods are the hallmarks of Japanese cuisine. Meals are ornate affairs steeped in tradition and ritual, with a variety of main courses served alongside boiled vegetables, pickles, and spice mixes– all offered in specially selected individual bowls. It is easy to see why when you look at Japan's environment. Encircled by the ocean, Japan's chain of mountainous islands is crisscrossed by rivers, and it was from these plentiful waterways that the Japanese captured fresh seafood, which is the centerpiece of most Japanese dinners.

The flavor of the fish is extremely important. Seasonality is also important whenever it comes to vegetables. As a result, the two important key values of Japanese food are flavor and variability. The third main quality of Japanese cuisine is elegance. Seasonal veggies are cleaned and gently cooked in liquid to bring out their delicate flavor. Also, dishes that take a long time to prepare are, on the whole, pleasing to the palate.

With these extinct flavors, "Japanese Cookbook" has a wide range of delicious Japanese recipes. It has four chapters with appetizers, snacks, breakfast, lunch, dinner, desserts, and Japan's most famous recipes. There is also a focus on sushi and ramen recipes. Read this book, follow these recipes, and have a flavorful, delicious meal every day.

Chapter 1: Introduction to Japanese Cuisine

Perfect presentation, tasty flavors, and healthy fresh ingredients are the hallmarks of Japanese cuisine. Meals are decorative activities, steeped in tradition and ceremony, with a variety of main courses served alongside fried rice, mustard, and spice mixes– all offered in specially selected individual bowls. Umami savories, which are commonly found in food products, are a distinctive Japanese flavor. The bonito seafood is processed to make 'katsuobushi,' which is then mixed with umami-rich shrimp or Kombu to make dashi or Japanese boiling stock. Another loved product is processed soybeans, which come as a result of white miso, red miso, and sesame oil, which are both used in condiments, sauces, and spice mixes.

Japan has a long tradition of veganism, with the exception of seafood, which is mostly consumed raw as seafood or sushi, thanks to its Buddhist origins. In the early 1900s, Japan's diet started to change with the introduction of beef and the incorporation of foreign cooking methods. Tonkatsu is based on a Viennese schnitzel and miso, which utilizes the European process of smashing and deep-frying, which are now part of modern Japanese cuisine. Japanese cuisine refers to the country's ethnic and cultural foods, which have evolved through decades of political, technological, and cultural progress. The standard Japanese cuisine consists of rice, fried rice, and other foods, focusing on new flavors. Salmon, marinated vegetables, and potatoes cooked in broth are popular food items. Seafood is widely available, and it is often fried, but it is often eaten raw as seafood or in salmon. Tempura refers to the deep-frying of seafood and vegetables in a soft batter.

Pasta, such as udon and soba, are staples in addition to rice. Many fermented dishes exist in Japan, like oden (salmon in broth) or nikujaga and sukiyaki (meat). Japanese culture has been influenced by Asian food in the past, but it has given up to Western delicacies in the modern period. Foods influenced by foreign cuisines, especially Chinese cuisine, such as ramen and gyoza, and also spaghetti, barbecue, and hamburgers, have been adapted to Japanese flavors and recipes. Due to various Buddhism, the Japanese also historically avoided meat, but since the late 19th century, meat-based recipes such as bulgogi and beef noodle soup have become popular. The popularity of Japanese cuisine, especially sushi, has spread across the globe.

1.1 History of Japanese Cuisine

With heavy influences from both Korea and China, Japanese cuisine has been there for over a thousand years. However, it's only been a few years before many of these influences have coalesced into what is now recognized as Japanese food. Rice from Asia was one of the main influences on Japan's main food in just over a century since 500 B.C. Rice was later utilized not only for feeding but also for making paper, wine, and other items. Though rice originated in Korea, soybean oil and wheat originated in China and have since been an important part of Japanese cuisine.

In Europe, dairy products aren't as common as they are in Japan. Between the ninth and fourteenth centuries, the first Japanese milk product known to the world was developed. Livestock was often developed solely for the purpose of pulling carts or plow fields. It was a long-forgotten tradition to use them for beef or even dairy until lately. Using them for beef, or even milk was a farfetched tradition until quite recently.

Spice use was also limited due to a shortage of meat products. Pepper and garlic were identified as early as the seventh century and were introduced from South Asia, either by China or personally. Garlic was often cultivated on a tiny level. However, these herbs were mostly used in the manufacture of medications and makeup.

Fish was an important substitution for meat due to the shortage of meat, and as an island country, this supply of food was plentiful, influencing many of today's most popular recipes. Prior to the advent of modern distribution systems, though, the complexity of storing and exporting fresh aquatic fish reduced demand in inland regions, where seasonal fish are widely consumed instead.

Sushi was born out of the practice of fermenting fish in boiling rice to preserve it. Anaerobic fermentation, which inhibits the growth of bacteria that cause putrefaction, preserves salted and inserted in rice fish. This older form of sushi is still made in western Japan near Lake Biwa, and related varieties can now be found in Asia, northeastern China, and East Asia. In reality, the strategy is believed to have started as a preservation method for freshwater fish captured in the Mekong River and it spread to Japan along with crop production.

The four seasons and nature continue to have a strong influence on Japanese cuisine nowadays. The most common foods are fish and veggies. Although the food can seem dull to some western people, the value of freshness, appearance, and taste balance cannot be overstated.

1.2 History of Traditional Dishes of Japanese Food

Other culture's cuisines have inspired Japanese food, but it has adapted and developed them to establish its own distinct food culture and food choices. About 350 B.C., China was the very first foreign intervention on Japan when the Japanese learned to grow rice. Chopsticks were invented in China, as was the use of sesame oil and soybean curd.

Another significant influence on the Japanese diet was Buddhism, which is among the two main religions in Japanese history. The advent of Buddhism in the 7th century lead to a ban on consuming meat. As a consequence of the prohibition, the famous dish sushi (smoked salmon with rice) was founded. Cooking patterns became more straightforward in the 19th century. Using one of five traditional cooking methods, a wide range of vegan (non - meat) products were prepared in tiny quantities. All foods were grouped into five color classes (yellowish, red, orange, white, and dark) and six flavor groups (bitter, salty, sweet, hot, sour, and delicate). The Japanese still use the same method of cooking.

Foreign trade started introducing foreign ideas to Japan in the early 12th century. The Dutch also added bread, cabbage, and potatoes. The Portuguese created the tempura. Mostly during Meiji Era, beef was allowed to return to Japan after such a thousand-year prohibition. Cake, tea, and frozen yogurt, among other food items, became popular in the late nineteenth century. The advent of time-saving flavor combinations is another Western influence. The electronic rice cooker is one of them, as are frozen foods like pot noodles, quick miso soup, and fast fermenting mixes. The Japanese, on the other hand, remain committed to their traditional cooking methods.

1.3 Nutritional Information and Benefits of Japanese Food

The Japanese diet is focused on the idea of prosperity and good health. Japanese cuisine is not only delicious and enticing, but it also has a range of health benefits. Unprocessed ingredients, added sugar or products, and large quantities of fruit and legumes are all part of traditional Japanese cuisine. Here are only a few of the many health advantages of eating Japanese food:

Certain Cancers

Hormone-dependent tumors, such as breast and cervical cancer, are highly rare in Japan. This is due to a higher intake of grains, oils, healthier fats, high-fiber products, and a reduced average calorie intake.

Large Variety

The Japanese diet includes a wide variety of vegetables that are high in important minerals that help with overall health. Seaweed, for instance, is very nutritious, containing significant quantities of iodine that can aid in the maintenance of a stable thyroid. Fruit, rich in fiber and moisture content, is also eaten in large quantities for lunch and desserts.

Heart Problems

Japan has one of the lowest levels of cardiovascular disease growth in the region and much lower as compared to developing countries. The Japanese diet is full of foods that can help support heart health, which explains why there are very few cases of heart disease.

Teas

Tea, which has various health benefits, is commonly served with Japanese dinners. Green tea has been shown to help reduce blood pressure, strengthen the immune system, lower cholesterol, and delay the aging process. It also has half the antioxidants in coffee and aids in the breakdown of oils in the digestive tract. Green tea's high antioxidant content also aids in the development of a calm and concentrated mental state.

Protein
The Japanese people recognize that consuming high-quality protein products contributes to a healthy lifestyle. Several of the recipes in Japanese cuisine are high in protein, which is very good for health. Some of the most popular classics in Japanese cuisine include seafood, poultry, and even tofu. When you consume a meal of protein, the bones, organs, tissue, skin, and even the plasma get healthier. Protein also contains a lot of iron, which helps keep the blood oxidized to begin to pump as quickly as possible.

1.4 Key ingredients of Japanese Food

Many Japanese recipes have delicately blended flavors, but the flavoring that gives them their complexity are normally made from the same ingredients.

Mirin
Mirin is a soft rice wine that is used to give dishes a touch of flavor. It's mostly used in soup supplies and dumpling stuffing blends.

Soy Sauce
One of the most basic flavorings in Japanese food is soy sauce. To give savory flavor to Japanese cuisine, soy sauce is used instead of salt.

Flakes of Bonito
Bonito is a small fish variety that is dried and trimmed into thin flakes that are used as the foundation for many Japanese sauces.

Rice Vinegar
Rice wine vinegar is used to spice rice.

Togarashi Shichimi

Shichimi Togarashi is a sweet chili powder blend with a blow.

Sushi Rice
Sushi rice is versatile rice that can be used in a variety of Japanese dishes. The grain is small, and when baked, it becomes oily and floury.

Nori
Nori is a kind of dried seaweed that can be eaten.

Wakame
Wakame is a kind of seaweed that is commonly used in Japanese food.

Kombu
Another component of Japanese dashi stocks is Kombu. It's a dry seaweed kelp that the Japanese grow for a unique taste.

Wasabi
Wasabi is a horseradish sauce made from a Japanese blend.

Miso Paste
Miso Paste is made from processed soybeans and is often combined with sea salt and rice to form a paste.

Noodles
Soba and udon noodles are famous because of their taste and color.

Chapter 2: Japanese Appetizers Recipes

2.1 Japanese Deviled Eggs

Cooking Time: 55 minutes
Serving Size: 18

Ingredients:
- 2 tablespoons green onions
- 4 tablespoons panko bread crumbs
- 2 teaspoons wasabi paste
- 2 teaspoons rice wine vinegar
- 9 eggs
- ½ cup mayonnaise
- 2 teaspoons soy sauce
- 2 tablespoons sesame seeds

Method:
1. In a saucepan, crack the eggs and fill them with water.
2. Bring to a boil, turn off the heat and set the eggs in hot water for a few minutes.
3. Remove the eggs from the hot water and position them under cold running water to cool before peeling.
4. In a dry medium bowl, cook and mix sesame seeds until nicely browned.
5. Transfer to a plate filled with a towel to cool.
6. Break each egg in half and combine the yolks with mayonnaise, wasabi paste, soy sauce, and garlic powder in a mixing bowl.
7. Place spring onions and panko crust crumbs in the yolk mixture and pump just enough to combine uniformly.

8. Place the egg white sections on a serving platter and spoon the yolk mixture into them.
9. Toss with sesame seeds that have been toasted.

2.2 Japanese Beef Tataki Rolls

Cooking Time: 20 minutes
Serving Size: 24 rolls
Ingredients:
- 2 teaspoon sesame seeds
- Large bunch cilantro
- 1 green
- 2 red chilies
- ¼ napa cabbage
- 1 carrot
- 1 lb. beef filet
- 1 tablespoon sesame oil
- 1 teaspoon sugar
- 4 tablespoon soy sauce
- 1 tablespoon neutral oil

Method:
1. Warm a nonstick or sheet iron frying pan over medium temperature until it is smoking hot.
2. Sear the beef fillet for 40 seconds on either side after brushing it with the neutral spray.
3. In a small cup, combine the sesame oil, soy sauce, glucose and whisk until the sugar has melted.
4. Transfer two tablespoons of the seasoning to the meat and rub it on.
5. Save the remaining dressing for the day.
6. Refrigerate the meat for at least an hour after wrapping it in glad tape.
7. Thinly slice the napa lettuce, cabbage, spring onions, and red chili.

8. Slice the beef finely and place a portion of each vegetable in the center.
9. Sprinkle a little of the coating on each roll before gently rolling it up.
10.   Serve hot with sesame seeds.

2.3 Japanese Rumaki

Cooking Time: 15 minutes
Serving Size: 8
Ingredients:
- 1 teaspoon fresh ginger
- 1 tablespoon brown sugar
- 4 small chicken livers
- 8 dash soy sauce
- 8 medium canned water chestnuts
- 4 slice bacon

Method:
1. Preheat the oven to 400 degrees Fahrenheit.
2. Place bacon on a sheet pan and bake for ten minutes, or until cooked and not crispy.
3. Remove the skillet from the pan and drain any excess fat before blotting the bacon and the skillet with paper towels.
4. In the center of each slice of bacon, put 1 liquid chestnut and half a grilled chicken.
5. Top each liver with a drop of soy sauce, ginger touch, and a sprinkling of brown sugar.
6. Use a skewer, protect the bacon around the water chestnuts and livers.
7. Transfer the pan to the oven and roast until the bacon is crispy and fluffy.

2.4 Japanese Sandwich Bites

Cooking Time: 5 minutes
Serving Size: 8
> **Ingredients:**
> - 4 whole cherry tomato
> - 8 toothpicks
> - 1-2 slices roasted turkey
> - 8 drops kewpie mayo
> - 8 cubes mild cheese
> - 1 Persian cucumber

Method:
1. Gather all of the necessary ingredients.
2. With a peeler, remove the skin of the Persian cucumber.
3. Make eight slices, each about ½ inch wide.
4. Use 8 cubes of cheese, split the cucumbers on edge.
5. Break 2 strips of roasted turkey into 1″ thick slices.
6. Each strip should be rolled up and placed on top of the cheese.
7. Squeeze a little amount of Kewpie Mayo over the turkey.
8. Put a toothpick through the middle top of each tomato after slicing it in half.
9. Use a toothpick, collect tomatoes and insert them into each turkey/cucumber mix.

2.5 Salmon Cucumber Tartare Bites

Cooking Time: 50 minutes
Serving Size: 4
> **Ingredients:**

For Serving
- Finely minced scallions
- Black sesame seeds optional
- Japanese seven flavor chili pepper
- 1 English cucumber

Salmon Tartare
- 1 teaspoon mirin
- ½ teaspoon sesame oil
- 2 teaspoons scallions
- 1 teaspoon soy sauce
- ½ pound fresh salmon fillet

Method:
1. Combine the salmon, green onions, sesame oil, mirin, and soy sauce in a medium mixing dish.
2. Cucumber ends should be trimmed.
3. Use a knife, score the cucumber skin laterally.
4. To serve, spoon Salmon Tartare into cucumber circles and marinade with Ichimi Togarashi and white sesame seeds.
5. Serve right away.

2.6 Cucumber Sunomono

Cooking Time: 1 hour 15 minutes
Serving Size: 5

Ingredients:
- 1 teaspoon salt
- 1 ½ teaspoons ginger root
- ⅓ cup rice vinegar

- 4 teaspoons white sugar
- 2 large cucumbers, peeled

Method:
1. Cucumbers should be split in half lengthwise, and any big seeds should be scooped out.
2. Cut into very small pieces crosswise.
3. Combine the vinegar, starch, salt, and seasoning in a shallow cup. Mix well.
4. Put cucumbers in the cup and swirl to cover them with the solution evenly.
5. Before eating, chill the cucumber dish for at least 1 hour.

Chapter 3: Japanese Breakfast Recipes

3.1 Japanese Fish Waffles

Cooking Time: 55 minutes
Serving Size: 6
Ingredients:
- 240g sweet red bean paste

Taiyaki Batter
- 1/3 cup milk
- 1 large egg
- 2 teaspoon baking powder
- 1/3 cup water
- 1½ tablespoon sugar
- 1 cup plain flour

Method:
1. In a big mixing cup, mix the flour and cornstarch and create a well in the middle.
2. Combine all of the milk mixtures and mix them into the flour properly.
3. Mix them, but do not overdo them.
4. Cover the bowl with cling wrap and chill for 30 minutes to allow the mixture to rest.
5. Over reduced temperature, steam the taiyaki pan and add around two tablespoons batter down the plate's bottom.
6. Pour the mixture from the pan's upper portion, allowing it to run with the ball down to the floor.
7. Position a roll of sweet red bean paste in the middle and drizzle with more powder (about two tablespoons).
8. Heat for five minutes on either side over low heat, pressing the plate.
9. Pick the Taiyaki cautiously until both sides have fried.

10.   Carry on for the rest of the batter and in the same way.

3.2 Japanese Pancakes

Cooking Time: 40 minutes
Serving Size: 8 pancakes
Ingredients:
- Nonstick cooking spray
- Maple syrup, for serving
- 3 large egg whites
- ¼ teaspoon cream of tartar
- ½ teaspoon pure vanilla extract
- 1 large egg yolk
- 1½ cups all-purpose flour
- 1¼ cups milk
- 4 tablespoons unsalted butter
- 2 teaspoons baking powder
- ½ teaspoon kosher salt
- 3 tablespoons confectioners' sugar

Method:
1. In a big mixing cup, combine the flour, butter flavoring' sugar, brown sugar, and salt.
2. In a medium mixing cup, whisk together all the milk, cream cheese, vanilla, and egg white until smooth.
3. In a separate big mixing cup, beat the eggs and icing sugar with an immersion blender at moderate speed for 2 minutes or until rigid peaks form.
4. Mix the flour mixture into the butter mixture (a few lumps are fine).
5. One-third of the pounded egg whites should be incorporated into the flour mix.

6. Double in the leftover egg whites until they are just mixed.
7. Use nonstick cooking oil, lightly coat the insides of four 3-inch-wide by 2-½ -inch-high circle molds.
8. Heat a big nonstick pan over medium heat, coated with cooking spray.
9. Cover each of the ready ring molds with ½ cup of powder and position them in the center of the pan.
10. Cover the pan with a cap and cook over medium heat or until the batter has risen to the ring molds' tops and is crispy on the rim.
11. Then use a spoon, loosen the bottoms of the pancakes.
12. To secure the ring molds, grab the side with tweezers and rotate them cautiously.
13. Cover and simmer for another five minutes, or until crispy on the other hand.
14. Break the mold and move to a tray.
15. Serve with a dollop of butter and a drizzle of maple syrup.
16. Before the cakes dampen, they must be served.
17. Repeat the cooking process with the leftover batter, lightly spraying the ring molds and coating the pan with nonstick cooking oil.

3.3 Japanese Milk Bread

Cooking Time: 50 minutes
Serving Size: 16 slices
Ingredients:
For the Tangzhong

- 6 tablespoon water
- 2 tablespoon bread flour

For the Rest of Loaf
- 3 tablespoon sugar
- 1 egg
- 30g unsalted butter
- 1 teaspoon salt
- 2 teaspoon fast acting yeast
- 120 ml milk ½ cup
- 300g bread flour

Method:
1. In a shallow saucepan, combine the water and grain for the tangzhong.
2. After switching on the oven, blend until smooth, and no chunks remain.
3. Heat the flour mixture gently on medium-low pressure, stirring continuously, till it hardens.
4. When you swirl it, you can see trails formed by the spatula.
5. Remove the pan from the heat and set it aside to cool.
6. In a big mixing dish, combine the rest of the ingredients (milk, yeast, flour, sugar, melted butter, salt, and egg).
7. Insert the cooled tangzhong.
8. Combine all of the components in a blender, then knead by hand on a baking sheet. If necessary, insert some more flour.
9. Move the dough to a finely oiled bowl until it is no longer messy.
10. Cover and set aside to rise in a warm location until doubled, approximately 1 hour.
11. Knock-back the flour and slice it into three parts until it has grown.
12. Place the remaining pieces to the sides and from one into a sphere.

13.   Stretch one part of the bread midway over the available dough, then spread the other half on top, creating three levels.
14.   If necessary, lightly rub the ball of bread, then roll it up like a cinnamon roll.
15.   Cover and set aside to climb until the loaf is just above the pan's rim.
16.   Preheat the oven to 350 degrees Fahrenheit/175 degrees Celsius.
17.   Clean the top of the bread with egg wash after lightly beating the egg.
18.   Preheat the oven to 350°F and bake the loaf for thirty minutes, or until lightly browned.
19.   If it starts to brown too quickly, tent it with parchment for the last few minutes of preparation.
20.   Allow cooling on a wire rack before cutting.

3.4 Japanese Sweet Filled Pancakes

Cooking Time: 30 minutes
Serving Size: 2
   Ingredients:
- Vegetable oil (for frying)
- ¾ pound Anko
- 3 tablespoons water (or milk)
- 1 cup all-purpose flour (sifted two large eggs)
- ½ teaspoon baking soda
- 2/3 cup sugar

Method:
1. Collect the required ingredients.
2. In a mixing cup, whisk together the eggs and sugar until smooth.
3. Baking soda can be dissolved in water.
4. In a separate bowl, whisk together the egg and water.

5. Gradually incorporate sifted flour into the beaten egg.
6. Lightly grease a pan or hot tray and steam it.
7. Create a small pancake with a scoop of flour in the pan (about 2 to 3 inches in measurement).
8. When bubbles emerge on the bottom, turn it over.
9. With each pancake, repeat the procedure.
10. Allow the pancakes to cool.
11. Grab a pair of pancakes with a handful of Anko sweet bean in the center.
12. Serve Immediately.

3.5 Japanese Green Tea Rice

Cooking Time: 15 minutes
Serving Size: 2
Ingredients:
- Some thinly sliced scallions
- ½ teaspoon sesame seeds
- 2 tablespoons green tea leaves
- ¼ teaspoon salt, or to taste
- 1 cup water
- 1 cup cooked sushi

Method:
1. Take the water to a boil in a large saucepan.
2. Then insert the tea leaves and salt and remove them from the oven.
3. Allow ten minutes to pass.
4. Tea should be drained and filtered.
5. Remove the green leaves and toss them out.
6. Place the steamed rice in a big shallow bowl.
7. Cover with spring onions and sesame seeds.
8. Instantly pour the tea over the grain and eat.

3.6 Japanese Ogura Toast

Cooking Time: 13 minutes
Serving Size: 8
Ingredients:
- Margarine or butter
- 8 tablespoon whipped cream
- 8 tablespoon red bean paste
- 2 pieces white bread

Method:
1. Butter the white bread by cutting it into fourths and toasting it until crispy.
2. While the toast is still sweet, spread real cheese or butter on it.
3. On each bread square, spread one tablespoon bean paste powder and one tablespoon cream cheese.

3.7 Japanese Fruit Sandwich

Cooking Time: 10 minutes
Serving Size: 4
Ingredients:
- ¼ teaspoon vanilla extract
- 8 slices Japanese sandwich bread
- ½ pint heavy cream
- 3½ tablespoons milk
- 1 mango
- 14 strawberries

- 1 kiwi fruit

Method:
1. Cut the kiwifruit into ¾-inch thick circles after peeling and slicing it.
2. Remove the peel from the mango, remove the tapered ends, and cut it into ¾-inch wide batons.
3. Strawberry tops can be removed. If they are too big, cut them in half.
4. In a cold pan, whisk together the heavy cream, condensed milk, and vanilla essence until strong peaks emerge.
5. On four slices of toast, add an even surface of whipped cream.
6. Fruit should be put on top of the whipped cream.
7. Ensure they are arranged on the outside of the sandwich where you will split it so the fruit shows up equally.
8. More cream should be used to fill up the cracks between the berries, and then the fruit should be topped with an even coating of cream.
9. Take the crusts from the four remaining bits of toast and cover the sandwiches.
10. Cutting the sandwiches would be better if they are refrigerated for at least 1 hour.
11. Cut them in half or quarters until you are about to eat them.

3.8 Japanese Strawberry Sauce

Cooking Time: 20 minutes
Serving Size: 2 cups
Ingredients:
- 1 tablespoon cornstarch
- ¼ cup water
- ½ cup sugar

- 1 tablespoon lemon juice
- 2 cups fresh strawberries

Method:
1. In a mixing dish, smash 1 cup of hulled berries with a stick blender or pastry cutter.
2. Integrate mashed berries, cornflour, lime juice, and liquid in a medium saucepan.
3. Get the water to a medium boil.
4. Heat for ten minutes, stirring continuously, or until liquid has browned.
5. Remove from heat and whisk in 1 cup sliced diced strawberries that have been set aside.
6. Leave to cool completely before frozen or refrigerating.

3.9 Japanese Rolled Omelets

Cooking Time: 10 minutes
Serving Size: 1
Ingredients:
- An oil-soaked paper towel
- Grated daikon radish
- 1 teaspoon soy sauce
- 1 teaspoon mirin
- 1½ tablespoons homemade dashi
- 2 large eggs

Method:
1. Use spoons, beat eggs in a shallow saucepan until well mixed and no clear white's remains.
2. In a mixing bowl, combine the cooled dashi, miso, and soy sauce.
3. Heat the tamagoyaki pan to moderate.
4. Fill the plate with one-quarter of the beaten egg.
5. Start rolling when the egg has completely set on the bottom but is still partially damp on top.
6. Raise the rolled section with your chopsticks and allow the raw egg to run beneath it.
7. Cook for another five minutes, popping any big bubble that develops.
8. Place the tamagoyaki on a wooden sushi mat and grind it up firmly yet gently; set aside for three minutes.
9. Move tamagoyaki to a large dish and, if necessary, cut crosswise.

3.10 Japanese Street Crepes

Cooking Time: 15 minutes
Serving Size: 20 crepes

Ingredients:

- 1 tablespoon sugar
- Anything you like for fillings
- 1 and ¾ cups milk
- 30g melted butter
- 3 eggs
- 1 cup flour

Method:

1. In a mixing cup, sift together flour, sugar, and a touch of salt.
2. Combine the whites and half of the milk in a mixing bowl.
3. Using an electric mixer, beat until all chunks are gone.
4. Insert the remaining milk, along with the butter, and proceed again.
5. Let cool for 15-30 minutes at ambient temperature.
6. Pour a small amount into a preheated, non-stick frying pan and quickly tilt the pan to distribute the batter evenly.
7. Cook over medium-high heat until golden brown on the underneath.
8. Switch the crepe by lifting the ends of the crepe.
9. Mostly on the second side, cook for about thirty minutes.
10. Fill the crepes in whatever way you like.

3.11 Japanese Tamago Kake Gohan

Cooking Time: 50 minutes
Serving Size: 2
Ingredients:
- 1 scallion, finely chopped
- Sesame seeds, for sprinkling
- Extra-virgin olive oil
- 2 eggs
- Splashes of tamari
- 2 to 3 cups brown rice

Optional Toppings
- Avocado slices
- Roasted broccoli
- Microgreens
- Splash of rice vinegar
- Thinly sliced nori
- Japanese pickles
- Extra egg yolks

Method:
1. Divide the fried brown rice evenly into two pans.
2. Whereas the rice is still warm, crack one egg into each bowl and add a dash of tamari, stirring vigorously so that the egg softly heats as it covers the rice, giving the rice a fluffy texture.
3. Add spring onions, sesame seeds, and any other preferred toppings to each dish.
4. Serve with a layer of tamari for spice.

Chapter 4: Japanese Snack Recipes

4.1 Crispix Japanese Snack Bowl

Cooking Time: 5 minutes
Serving Size: 2
Ingredients:
- ½ packet mixed rice crackers
- A handful of black sesame seeds
- 50g of Wasabi hot peas
- 2 sheets of nori (seaweed)
- ½ cup Crispix

Method:
1. To make the lower part, place Kellogg's Crispix flakes in a small cup.
2. Transfer the wasabi peas to the mix.
3. Crumble the nori layers into the bowl after breaking them in half.
4. To give the bowl a little more bite, toss in some blended rice crackers.
5. Over the end, sprinkle the black sesame seeds.
6. Merge all components in a bowl and serve!

4.2 Easy Japanese Dorayaki Recipe

Cooking Time: 45 minutes
Serving Size: 6
Ingredients:
- 1 teaspoon neutral-flavored oil
- 1.1 lb. red bean paste
- 1 teaspoon baking powder
- 1-2 tablespoon water
- 4 large eggs
- 2 tablespoon honey

- 1 ⅓ cup all-purpose flour
- ⅔ cup sugar

Method:
1. Assemble all of the necessary ingredients.
2. Whisk together the eggs, honey, and sugar in a big mixing bowl until the combination becomes creamy.
3. Scroll together the powder and cornstarch in a mixing cup.
4. Refrigerate for 15 minutes to allow flavors to meld.
5. The batter can now be a little cleaner. Add 2 teaspoons of water.
6. Over moderate pressure, heat a big nonstick deep fryer.
7. Cover the bottom of the plate with a paper towel dipped in olive oil.
8. The oil could then be fully removed.
9. Pour 3 tablespoons of the batter into a spoon or a shallow measuring cup.
10. To avoid drying, move to a sheet and protect with a wet cloth.
11. Get a red bean paste sandwich.
12. In the middle, place the redder bean paste.

4.3 Homemade Senbei Rice Crackers

Cooking Time: 40 minutes
Serving Size: 4

Ingredients:
Senbei
- 2 tablespoon vegetable oil
- 4 tablespoon water
- 40g cooked white rice
- ¼ teaspoon sea salt
- 120g rice flour or mochiko

Glaze
- 2 teaspoon mirin
- 1 tablespoon soy sauce

Toppings
- 2 teaspoon red chili pepper mix
- Nori seaweed sheets
- 3 teaspoon black sesame seeds
- 5 teaspoon furikake rice

Method:
1. Preheat the oven to 190 degrees Celsius.
2. To make the glaze, whisk together the soy sauce and mirin.
3. In a mixing bowl, combine the corn starch, rice flour, salt, and oil to produce the pastry.
4. Run until the mixture is finely mixed.
5. Place the mixture in a bowl and insert your desired flavorings.
6. Remove the plastic from the dough 'disc' and place it on the prepared baking sheet.
7. Bake the pretzels for 8-10 minutes, one baking tray at a time.
8. Using a spatula, turn the pretzels.
9. Bake for 8-10 minutes more, or until the crackers begin to tan.
10. Brush the soy sauce and miso glaze over the tops.
11. Return to the oven and bake for another ten minutes or until well browned.
12. Before serving, cool full on a wire rack.

4.4 "Yamitsuki" Cabbage

Cooking Time: 25 minutes
Serving Size: 4
Ingredients:
- Korean sesame oil
- Sesame seeds
- Salt and pepper to taste
- ½ - 1 green cabbage

Method:
1. Make a rectangle out of the cabbage.
2. Place the cut cabbage in a mixing bowl, season with salt and pepper to taste, and toss to combine.
3. Drizzle 1-2 tablespoons of sesame oil over the cabbage and toss to combine.
4. As a finishing touch, scatter sesame seeds on top.

4.5 Cinnamon Flavored New Karinto

Cooking Time: 1 hour
Serving Size: 2
Ingredients:
- ½ teaspoon of cinnamon
- 1 tablespoon of water
- 1 egg
- 60 grams of sugar
- 100 grams of flour
- 1¼ teaspoon of salt
- 30 grams sliced almonds
- 1 teaspoon of cinnamon
- 1 tablespoon of sugar
- ½ teaspoon of baking powder

Method:

1. In a mixing cup, add all of the components and stir until well combined.
2. The egg should be thoroughly whisked before being added to the combination with a slotted spoon.
3. After allowing the dough to rest for thirty minutes, cover it in cling film and stretch it out to a width of 1-2 mm.
4. Split the noodles into pieces, then cut each slice into 5-cm sizes, as if they were soba noodles.
5. In 180°C oil, deep-fry the pieces.
6. When they change color and stop sizzling, they are done.
7. Drain all extra oil thoroughly.
8. In a casserole dish, warm the sugar, spice, and water until the sugar melts and becomes translucent.
9. Then add the deep-fried pieces, remove from the heat, and shake the pan to cover the sticks in the sugar.
10. Press them out onto a plate to cool as the sugar begins to harden and the texture of the sticks becomes powdery.

4.6 Homemade Pocky

Cooking Time: 1 hour 40 minutes
Serving Size: 12

Ingredients:

- 50g unsalted butter
- 3 tablespoon milk
- 150g plain flour

- A pinch of salt
- 1 tablespoon sugar

Topping Suggestions
- 2 tablespoon crushed almonds
- Milk chocolate

Method:

1. In a mixing bowl, combine all of the dry ingredients and pump one or two times.
2. In a mixing bowl, spin the sliced butter two to three times before it resembles rough bread crumbs.
3. Pulse in the milk once more.
4. Refrigerate the dough ball for thirty minutes after wrapping it in saran wrap.
5. Heat the oven to 180 degrees Celsius (350 degrees Fahrenheit).
6. Stretch out the dough to a thickness of around 5mm.
7. Break off the extra dough on the sides and turn it into a shape.
8. Then slice it into small strips.
9. Preheat the oven to 350°F and bake the pieces for fifteen minutes.
10. Cover with chocolate sauce and all other desired toppings.

Chapter 5: Japanese Lunch Recipes

5.1 Unagi Don Grilled Eel Rice Bowl

Cooking Time: 50 minutes
Serving Size: 1-2

Ingredients:
- 260ml water
- 2 eel fillets, skin-on
- 200g rice

Unagi Sauce
- 4 tablespoon soy sauce
- 4 tablespoon mirin
- 1 ½ tablespoon cooking sake
- 2 ½ tablespoon sugar

Method:
1. To prepare the sauce in a medium bowl, mix the mirin and sake and bring to the boil.
2. Turn off the heat and mix in the sugar until it is fully dissolved.
3. Bring to a simmer with soy sauce.
4. Lower the heat and continue to cook for another ten minutes.
5. Preheat your barbecue to medium temperature.
6. Rub the fillets with olive oil and place them on top.
7. Position the grilling machine on the barbecue and cook for 5-7 minutes.
8. Remove the fillets from the oven and clean them with the unagi sauce, saving some for later.
9. Return the fillets to the grilling machine and cook for another minute.
10. Transfer a helping of fried rice to an empty bucket to serve.

11. Brush the residual sauce over the rice and place the unagi on top.

5.2 Chirashi Chakin Sushi

Cooking Time: 55 minutes
Serving Size: 6
Ingredients:
- 2 tablespoons black sesame seeds
- 6 sprigs of Italian parsley
- 2 tablespoons white sugar
- 1 teaspoon salt
- 1 tablespoon vegetable oil
- 3 tablespoons rice vinegar
- 3 eggs, beaten
- ¼ teaspoon salt
- 1 cup sushi rice

Method:
1. Bring water to a boil in a casserole dish. Stir in the rice.
2. Spoon the rice into a big mixing bowl until it's done cooking.
3. In the meantime, whisk together the eggs and ¼ teaspoon of salt.
4. 1/6 of the egg mixture should be poured into the pan and spread uniformly.
5. Cook until the eggs have finally set somewhat.
6. In a small cup, combine vinegar, honey, and one teaspoon salt.
7. Reheat the combination for a few moments until it is warm.
8. In a warm bowl, combine the rice, vinegar, and green onions.
9. Place a big bowlful of rice in the middle of each egg layer to combine.

10.   To serve, turn into a round and connect with a sprig of Italian tarragon.

5.3 Unagi Hitsumabushi Grilled Eel Rice Bowl

Cooking Time: 50 minutes
Serving Size: 1

Ingredients:
- Wasabi paste
- Dashi stock
- Shredded nori seaweed
- Chopped spring onions
- 1 grilled unagi eel filet
- Japanese sansho pepper powder
- 160g fresh steamed rice

Unagi Sauce
- 2 tablespoon soy sauce
- 1 tablespoon honey
- 1 tablespoon sake
- 2 tablespoon mirin

Method:
1. In a pan over medium heat, combine all of the components for the unagi sauce.
2. Mix until the liquid has browned and is uniformly mixed.
3. Unagi fillets can be cut into short strips.
4. Pour some rice into a cup and finish with unagi sauce for the first serving.
5. Place the unagi pieces on top of the rice and drizzle with additional sauce.
6. Enjoy with a dash of sansho spice powder and nori.

5.4 Chanko Nabe Hot Pot

Cooking Time: 1 hour
Serving Size: 4-6
Ingredients:
- 1 piece dried kombu
- 1 tablespoon soy sauce
- 2 teaspoons white miso paste
- 4 cups chicken broth
- 2 garlic cloves
- 1 tablespoon ginger
- 4–6 large eggs
- 8 ounces maitake mushrooms
- 8 ounces udon noodles
- 3 tablespoons vegetable oil
- ¾ teaspoon kosher salt

Chicken Meatballs with Ginger and Miso
- 8 ounces large shrimp
- 2 tablespoons scallions
- 1 tablespoon rice wine vinegar
- 8 ounces flaky white fish
- ¾ pound baby bok choy
- 1 medium carrot

Method:
1. Cook udon as per box instructions in a small saucepan of hot, salted water.
2. Close the pot and bring boiling liquid back to a boil, then use eggs.
3. Cook, sometimes stirring, until the eggs are soft-boiled, around 6 minutes.
4. Sauté the mushrooms with the salt until they are finely browned, and the moisture has evaporated.
5. Stir in the garlic and ginger and simmer for 30–60 seconds, or until fragrant.
6. Mix in the pesto, then pour in the chicken stock.

7. If used, add the Kombu, soy sauce, and the leftover half teaspoon of salt.
8. Toss in the meatballs and vegetables.
9. For use, add the bok choy and vinegar.
10. Arrange the cod on top of the stew.
11. Cook, wrapped, until gently tossing in the shrimp.
12. Divide the stew between the pans. Lastly, add the scallions.

5.5 Kuri Kinton Chestnut and Sweet Potato Mash

Cooking Time: 40 minutes
Serving Size: 2

Ingredients:
- 1-2 teaspoon sugar, to taste
- 100g candied chestnuts in syrup
- 200g sweet potato

Method:
1. Break the sweet potato into even pieces after peeling it.
2. Cook until the potatoes are tender, about 10-15 minutes.
3. With a knife, check the softness.
4. Discharge and smash with half of the chestnuts once soft.
5. To finish, save one-half of a large chestnut.
6. Arrange the sugar and finely cut the leftover chestnuts.
7. Toss the mashed potato and chestnuts with the diced chestnuts and the reserved sauce.
8. Gently combine the ingredients.
9. Taste for flavor, and if possible, insert 1-2 teaspoons of sugar.

10.   Serve with the preserved chestnut on top.

5.6 New Year Soba (Toshikoshi Soba)

Cooking Time: 1 hour
Serving Size: 4
Ingredients:
Noodle Soup
- 1 tablespoon sugar
- 300ml tsuyu
- 100ml mirin
- 200ml soy sauce
- 1.5 liter bonito kelp dashi stock

Noodles
- 20g tempura flakes
- 150g kamaboko fish cake
- 100g spring onions
- 200g soba buckwheat noodles

Method:
1. Keep your dashi stock in a big pot. After that, insert the mirin and cook for a few minutes on low heat.
2. Before inserting the soy sauce, transfer the sugar and let it melt.
3. Bring 1 liter of water on the stove in a separate pot.
4. Add the soba and give it a gentle stir.
5. Turn down the heat to low heat and continue to cook for about ten minutes.
6. Discharge the noodles and wash them in cool water, softly rubbing the pasta's surface to remove any extra flour.
7. The spring vegetables and any other condiments can then be finely sliced.

8. Softly re-heat the stock and spill into tins, then add the pasta and garnish with your bell peppers and tempura granules.

5.7 Hayashi Rice Stew

Cooking Time: 1 hour 20 minutes
Serving Size: 4
Ingredients:
- 2 tablespoon sesame oil
- 800g cooked Japanese rice
- 1 carrot
- 100g fresh Asian mushrooms
- 200g finely sliced beef
- 450-500ml water
- 1 onion
- 1 teaspoon Worcestershire sauce
- 6-8 blocks Hayashi rice stew

Method:
1. Slice your vegetables and meat into bite-sized bits as your rice cooks.
2. Start by softening the veggies in one tablespoon of soy sauce in a heavy-bottomed pan until they are slightly sautéed.
3. Heat until the beef is golden brown.
4. Till the meat is heated through, add water and bring to a boil, reduce to low heat and let the mixture simmer for about fifteen minutes.
5. Remove the pan from the fire and stir in the Hayashi Rice Stew Roux.
6. Finally, reduce the heat to low and continue to cook for another ten minutes.
7. For extra spice, add a Worcestershire sauce.
8. Serve with a side of rice that has been baked.

5.8 Yakitori Grilled Skewers

Cooking Time: 1 hour 5 minutes
Serving Size: 1
Ingredients:
- Spring onions
- Chicken breast

Suggested Additional Items
- Asparagus
- Firm tofu
- Pork belly slices
- Green pepper
- Leek

Sauce
- 1-2 teaspoon katakuriko potato starch
- Shichimi pepper seasoning
- 3 tablespoon soy sauce
- 2 tablespoon sugar
- 1 tablespoon mirin
- 1 tablespoon cooking sake

Method:
1. In a bowl with two tablespoons of sugar, combine the boiling sake, miso, and sesame oil.
2. In a small saucepan, mix a little katakuriko rice flour in water and heat the mixture while boiling it.
3. Soak the wood dowels in water for a minute before using.
4. Begin spearing the components onto skewers.
5. Start glazing the slicer components with your yakitori sauces using a baking brush.
6. Begin by setting the skewers on the grill in an environment where the heat is high and even.

7. Switch the yakitori often to ensure even cooking, and sprinkle more yakitori sauces onto the meat each time.
8. The meat will be edible once it has turned golden brown.

5.9 Aji Nanbanzuke Spicy Horse Mackerel with Vegetables

Cooking Time: 2 hours
Serving Size: 2-3

Ingredients:
- Pinch of salt and pepper
- Oil for frying
- 2 bell peppers
- 3 tablespoon potato starch
- 1 onion
- 1 carrot
- 3 horse mackerel fillets

For the Marinade
- 1 ½ tablespoon soy sauce
- 1 red chili pepper
- 1 tablespoon mirin rice wine
- 1 tablespoon sake
- 50ml sushi vinegar

Method:
1. Red chili peppers can be cut into small rounds.
2. Merge all of the marinade ingredients in a mixing bowl and set aside.
3. Any of the veggies should be thinly sliced.
4. Place a small amount of oil in a deep fryer.
5. Sauté the veggies before they are tender and soft.
6. Remove the pan from the fire and insert the marinade, tossing gently.

7. Season the fillets on both sides with salt and pepper.
8. After that, gently coat in corn starch.
9. Preheat any cooking oil to 180°C in a frying pan.
10. Carefully place 1-2 fillets at the moment, skins down flat, into the oil, and cook until crispy.
11. Position the fillets on a pan, then spill the veggies and marinade over them.
12. For a complete dinner, serve with rice.

Chapter 6: Japanese Dinner Recipes

6.1 Takoyaki Octopus Balls

Cooking Time: 1 hour
Serving Size: 1-2

Ingredients:
Batter
- 450ml water
- Pinch of dashi stock powder
- 2 eggs
- 200g flour

Fillings
- Red pickled ginger
- Tempura flakes
- 1 bunch spring onion
- 100g fresh octopus

Toppings
- Aosa powdered seaweed
- Katsuobushi bonito flakes
- Japanese mayonnaise
- Takoyaki sauce

Method:
1. Begin by making the batter.
2. Combine eggs, flour, liquid, and just a little dashi stock in a big mixing cup.
3. Set this aside for now.
4. Octopus can be cut into small sections.
5. Put an octopus fragment in each of the semi-circular spaces.
6. Now you can fill each hole with minced green onion, red miso paste, and tempura flakes.
7. You will need to turn the takoyaki once they are around halfway fried, about 1-2 minutes.

8. It would take around 3-4 minutes for the outside to turn light golden.
9. Smother a few takoyaki on a tray with takoyaki liquid and Japanese mayo.

6.2 BBQ Pork Chashu

Cooking Time: 1 hour 20 minutes
Serving Size: 4-6
Ingredients:
- 2 pieces ginger
- 1 leek
- 110g sugar
- 2 cloves garlic
- 1.3kg pork belly
- 200ml cooking sake
- 50ml mirin
- 1-liter water
- 500ml soy sauce

Method:
1. Use the baker's rope, roll the pulled pork, leaving the skin on edge.
2. Parsley and spice can be roughly chopped and peeled.
3. Over low heat, combine the soy sauce, steam, boiling sake, mirin, honey, garlic, spice, and leek in a big pan.
4. After that, toss in the rolled pork belly.
5. Decrease to low, medium heat for 3-4 hours.
6. It is important to remember to boil it low and slow.
7. Allow cooling before marinating in the sauce night in the refrigerator.
8. Cover the pork with cling film after removing it from the liquid.

9. Serve ramen noodles, hot rice, or vegetables thinly sliced.

6.3 Sekihan Azuki Bean Rice

Cooking Time: 9 hours 5 minutes
Serving Size: 5

Ingredients:
- ½ teaspoon kosher salt
- Toasted black sesame seeds
- ½ cup Japanese rice
- 2 ½ cups water
- 3 cups sweet rice
- ½ cup azuki beans

Method:
1. In a cup, place the azuki beans.
2. Carry only enough water to bring the beans to boiling over moderate flame.
3. Return the azuki beans to the pot and add 2 ½ cup water.
4. By thoroughly mixing a bean between your two thumbs, you can tell if it is done.
5. Rinse both rice flour and Japanese short-grain rice completely in a mixing pan.
6. Fill the rice cooker bowl halfway with rice.
7. Put in the azuki-cooking water that has been set aside.
8. Finally, uniformly spread the beans on top, being careful not to combine them with the rice.
9. Serve the rice with a gentle stir.

6.4 Yakisoba Fried Noodles

Cooking Time: 50 minutes
Serving Size: 1

Ingredients:
- Pickled shredded ginger
- Dried bonito flakes
- 1 small carrot
- Aonori powdered seaweed
- ⅛ white cabbage
- ¼ green pepper
- 1 portion yakisoba noodles
- 50g pork
- ½ onion
- 1 tablespoon mayonnaise
- 2 tablespoon yakisoba sauce

Method:
1. Slice the pork into thin portions to start.
2. Carrots and peppers should be thinly sliced, and cabbage and onion should be finely chopped.
3. Cover until the pork is golden brown, add the remaining veggies (excluding the cabbage), and bake until they are tender.
4. After the other veggies are finished, insert the cabbage.
5. Toss the pasta in the pan with the yakisoba sauce and stir to combine.
6. Spray over aonori and cover with sliced pickled ginger until it is finished.
7. You should incorporate dried bonito chips and mayo for extra flavor.

6.5 Karaage Japanese Fried Chicken

Cooking Time: 45 minutes
Serving Size: 4

Ingredients:

- ½ teaspoon black pepper
- Lemon wedge
- 1 cup potato starch
- ¼ teaspoon fine sea salt
- 4 skin-on chicken thighs
- Peanut oil
- 1 ½ teaspoons fresh ginger
- 3 tablespoons soy sauce
- 2 teaspoons sugar
- 2 tablespoons dry sake
- 2 teaspoons grated garlic

Method:

1. Merge the garlic, ginger, rice, sesame oil, and sugar in a small baking dish big enough to hold the meat.
2. Preheat the oil to 350 degrees Fahrenheit.
3. Place a sheet pan over a separate cookie sheet as the oil gets hot.
4. Combine rice flour, salt, and peppers in a mixing cup.
5. Fry three or four bits at a time, maintaining a 325°F oil temperature.
6. Cook for about three minutes.
7. Double the temperature of the oil to 375 degrees until all of the chicken has been cooked once.
8. Serve with a lemon slice, spinach, and cottage cheese, warm or at ambient temperature.

6.6 Kurigohan (Chestnut Rice)

Cooking Time: 45 minutes
Serving Size: 6
Ingredients:
- 1 tablespoon soy sauce
- Black sesame seeds
- 1 tablespoon sake
- 1 tablespoon mirin
- 400g Japanese short-grain rice
- 600 ml water
- 400g jarred Kuri chestnuts
- 50g sweet mochi rice

Method:
1. Wash and drain the rice immediately.
2. In a big mixing bowl, combine all rice and rinse with ice water until the water flows clean.
3. In a big pan, mix the rice, liquid, sake, miso, and sesame oil.
4. Bring to a boil, then shield and decrease to low heat for around 20 minutes, just until the rice consumes the water.
5. Remove the rice from the heat source.
6. The chestnuts are then added and covered with a cap for ten minutes to heat up.
7. Serve in bowls of black sesame seeds on top and eat.

6.7 Tekone Sushi Marinated Tuna Rice Bowl

Cooking Time: 1 hour 10 minutes

Serving Size: 4

Ingredients:
- 3 tablespoon soy sauce
- Sushi rice for four people
- 1 tablespoon mirin
- 1 tablespoon cooking sake
- 500g sashimi grade raw tuna

To Serve
- Sushi ginger
- 2 tablespoon nori seaweed
- 1 tablespoon sesame seeds
- 3 shiso perilla leaves

Method:
1. In a shallow saucepan, combine the mirin, boiling sake, and sesame oil and heat over medium heat.
2. Turn down the heat to moderate and boil for around five minutes until it begins to simmer.
3. Enable the marinade to cool, then use.
4. Cut the tuna into little bite-size bits, and blend it with the marinade in a mixing bowl.
5. Enable thirty minutes in the refrigerator to marinate.
6. You may now prepare your sushi rice.
7. When the sushi rice is finished, divide it into two bowls with the salmon that has been marinated.
8. Cut the shiso perilla plants into small slices and scatter the herbs, green onions, and sushi spice on the side of the cups.

6.8 Shogayaki Ginger Pork

Cooking Time: 20 minutes
Serving Size: 2

Ingredients:
- 1 tablespoon neutral-flavored oil

- 1 green onion
- Kosher salt
- Freshly ground black pepper
- ½ lb. thinly sliced pork loin
- 1 clove garlic
- 1 knob ginger
- ¼ onion

Seasonings
- 2 tablespoon sake
- 1 teaspoon sugar
- 2 tablespoon mirin
- 2 tablespoon soy sauce

Method:
1. Gather all of the necessary ingredients.
2. Grate the onion and ginger into a shallow dish. Garlic can be minced.
3. Season with salt and pepper.
4. Use salt and black pepper, spice the beef.
5. Heat the oil in a big nonstick pan over medium heat.
6. Brown the chicken in a thin layer in a frying skillet, turning until the bottom is nicely browned.
7. Cook in batches to ensure that the beef is adequately seared without boiling. Just sure the bacon is not overcooked.
8. Include the ingredients and sliced scallion until all sides are neatly seared. Serve right away.

6.9 Zaru Tray Udon Noodles with Dipping Sauce

Cooking Time: 40 minutes
Serving Size: 1
Ingredients:
- Mentsuyu soup base

- Udon

Suggested Toppings
- Grated daikon
- Wasabi paste
- Ginger
- Green onions
- Nori seaweed strips
- Ground sesame seeds

Method:

1. Start preparing your udon noodles according to the box directions.
2. After frying, immediately rinse them under cool water to ensure that the noodles maintain their chewiness.
3. Drain the noodles full until they have cooled.
4. Put the noodles on a zaru sheet and set them aside.
5. Dilute the mentuyu as per the instructions on the container.
6. Serve with a variety of toppings.

Chapter 7: Japanese Desserts Recipes

7.1 Manju, Japanese Steamed Cake

Cooking Time: 30 minutes
Serving Size: 10
Ingredients:

- Cake flour for dusting
- Frying oil
- 60ml water
- 250g red bean paste
- 120g cake flour
- 40g granulated sugar
- 4g baking powder

Method:
1. Assemble all of the necessary ingredients.
2. Combine water and brown sugar in a shallow frying pan.
3. Over moderate pressure, swirl to melt the sugar.
4. Allow cooling in a big mixing bowl.
5. In the meantime, wet your hands with just a little liquid and shape 12 red bean powder balls.
6. Integrate baking powder and liquid in a mixing bowl.
7. Put all together in the cooling brown flour mix.
8. Mix the flour into the brown sugar solution and blend to combine.
9. Make a ball out of the clumps by pinching them together.
10. Fill a bowl with bubble wrap and set it aside for fifteen minutes to stabilize the dough.
11. Make the dough for 1 to 2 minutes on a floured surface.
12. Shape the dough into a roll and cut until it is no more sticky and flat.

13. To save the flour from drying out, cover it with a wet towel.
14. To cover the dough, position the bean paste ball in the center and push each corner into the middle.
15. Get a steamer. Two inches of water should be added to the skillet.
16. Get the mixture to a boil in a large pot. Use high fire, boil for 10-12 minutes.
17. Take the manju from the container and chill on a cutting board or bamboo sieve until they have finished cooking.

7.2 Strawberry Mochi

Cooking Time: 25 minutes
Serving Size: 6
Ingredients:
- 180g sweet white bean paste
- 6 medium-sized strawberry
- 200ml water
- Katakuriko potato starch
- 30g sugar
- 180g Shiratamako

Method:
1. Remove the stems from the berries and wash them.
2. Put a strawberry in the middle of the white bean mixture and straighten it.
3. Make a round ball out of the strawberry by wrapping it in white bean paste.
4. In a big heatproof bowl, combine Shiratamako and sugar, then add more water.
5. Mix and combine thoroughly.
6. Reheat for another minute after stirring well with a dough scraper.
7. Load the mochi cup onto the starch and sprinkle ample Karakuriko on the rolling pad.
8. Split the mochi into five sections and roll each one out flat to a diameter of around 10 cm.
9. Position the strawberry covered in white bean paste on the stretched-out mochi.
10. Using well-dusted paws, collect the surface of the mochi covering and wrap the berries in it.
11. With your well-dusted hand, cover the mochi edges at the bottom and turn it into a good round daifuku mochi.

12.   Toss in the leftover mochi and berries and
continue the cycle.

7.3 No-Bake Crème Caramel

Cooking Time: 50 minutes
Serving Size: 8
Ingredients:
Caramel Sauce
- 2 tablespoon water
- 2 tablespoon boiling water
- ⅔ cup sugar

Custard
- ½ cup heavy cream
- 2 teaspoon pure vanilla extract
- 80g sugar
- 1¾ cups whole milk
- ¼ cup water
- 4 large egg yolks
- 4 sheets gelatin powder

Method:
1. Assemble all of the necessary ingredients.
2. In a small saucepan, mix the water and sugar.
3. Gently stir and rotate the pan again to evenly disperse the solution.
4. Remove the pan from the heat and place it on a cool, damp towel before adding boiling water.
5. Heat the ramekins in warm water for a few seconds.
6. Allocate the caramel equally among the eight ramekins while it is still sweet.
7. Break four gelatin plates into small slices in a shallow bowl.
8. Put down for 5-6 minutes after adding 14 cups of cold water.
9. Begin dissolving the gelatin by placing the container of gelatin solution over the frying pan.

10. Remove the pan from the fire and set it aside.
11. Mix the egg whites and sugar in a big bowl and mix until light and fluffy.
12. Heat dairy in a small saucepan until it becomes hot to the touch.
13. Slowly drizzle in the wet milk.
14. Re-insert the solution into the frying pan.
15. Cook, moving continuously, over medium-low pressure.
16. Mix up the gelatin solution thoroughly. Switch off the heat.
17. Then use a fine-mesh colander, pour the mixture into a small bowl.
18. Fill the ramekins halfway with the custard.

7.4 Shiratama Dango

Cooking Time: 12 minutes
Serving Size: 16
Ingredients:
Mochiko
- 2 ½ tablespoon water
- ½ teaspoon sugar
- ⅓ cup mochiko
Shiratamako
- 3 tablespoon water
- ½ teaspoon sugar
- ⅓ cup shiratamako

Method:
1. Assemble all of the necessary ingredients.
2. In a big mixing cup, mix mochiko, honey, and 2 tablespoons of water.
3. With a stick blender, combine it until it's almost smooth.

4. Shape a ball out of the mochiko combination by pressing it with your fist.
5. Slowly drizzle in the remaining ½ tablespoon water when shaping a ball.
6. Collect crumbs in the cup with the mochiko ball in this manner.
7. The dough should have the feel of an earlobe, according to instructions.
8. Then turn into a flat surface, which you can then shape into a log.
9. Squeeze off dough pieces from the logs and roll it into a 34-inch ball, then fold into a 12-inch-thick disc.
10. You must be able to get about 16 balls out from this method.
11. Create an incision in the middle with your index finger.
12. Heat the shiratama dango for two minutes in hot water.
13. Collect the shiratama dango as they begin to move and dunk them in ice water to cool.

7.5 Strawberry Awayukikan Dessert

Cooking Time: 40 minutes
Serving Size: 2-3
Ingredients:
- 1 egg white
- 50g sugar

- 300ml water
- 4g powdered kanten
- 5 strawberries

Method:
1. Take the stalks from the berries and wash them.
2. Then, using a fork, mash three berries and slice the remaining berries thinly for decorations.
3. Set aside the cut berries for a later point.
4. In a moderate saucepan, combine the water and flavoring and bring to a boil over medium heat.
5. When it begins to simmer, reduce the heat to low and continue to swirl until the gelatin has fully dissolved.
6. In a frying pan, combine the mashed berries and sugars and mix well.
7. Enable to solidify at room temperature after turning off the heat.
8. Stir the egg whites in a large bowl until stiff peaks emerge, then gradually applying the egg whites' gelatin solution.
9. Place the cut strawberries on the top of a jar lined with parchment.
10. Then spill the combination over the strawberries and place in the fridge to cool until solid.
11. Take the cake out of the bowl when about to eat and turn it over, so the strawberry pieces are on edge.
12. Cut into two to three parts. As a light snack or a substitute for marshmallows, try this method.

7.6 Anmitsu

Cooking Time: 1 hour
Serving Size: 3
Ingredients:
- 3 tablespoon sugar
- 1-2 tablespoon azuki bean paste
- 400ml water
- 1 teaspoon matcha powder
- 4g Kanten powder

For the Syrup
- 50-80ml water
- 2 tablespoon sugar

Method:
1. In a shallow saucepan or cup, combine the matcha powder and sugars and set it aside.
2. In a frying pan, combine the water, kanten material, and matcha syrup combination and bring to the boil over medium-high heat, stirring constantly.
3. Stir occasionally for a few seconds or until all of the ingredients have dissolved.
4. Turn off the heat and set it aside for ten minutes to cool.
5. Fill a container halfway with the combination.
6. Enable 2-3 hours in the refrigerator to set.
7. To create the syrup, combine the sugar and water in a frying pan and cook over medium heat until the sugar is fully dissolved.
8. Allow the sugar to cool after it has melted.
9. Slice the matcha gelatin into pieces and place them in a pie dish with the azuki paste on top.
10. Over the gelatin and azuki powder, add the syrup and serve.

Chapter 8: Japanese Sushi Recipes

8.1 Sushi Rolls Futomaki

Cooking Time: 10 minutes
Serving Size: 3 sushi rolls

Ingredients:
- 2 tablespoon sake
- 2 tablespoon soy sauce
- 1 cup dried shiitake mushrooms
- 2 tablespoon sugar
- 3 seaweed nori sheets
- ½ cucumber
- 1/3 packet Kanpyo
- 1 rolled egg tamagoyaki
- ½ carrot
- 4.5 cups of sushi rice

Method:
1. Cook and prepare the sushi rice.
2. Wash the mushrooms in hot distilled water in a pan.
3. Drench Kanpyo in 1 cup of water in a different bowl.
4. Start preparing the cucumber, carrot, potato, and tamagoyaki.
5. Try squeezing the extra liquid from the mushrooms into a cup and finely dice them.
6. In a frying pan, combine the soaked mushroom broth, sugar, steak, and soy sauce.
7. Bring to a simmer, then decrease to medium heat and continue to cook until much of the fluid has evaporated, and the vegetables are tender.
8. Arrange the fillings in the sushi rice's middle.

9. Transfer a small amount of water to the greater edge of the seaweed and roll it.

8.2 Vegetable Sushi

Cooking Time: 1 hour 20 minutes
Serving Size: 20 rolls
Ingredients:
For the Rice
- 3 tablespoons sugar
- Salt
- 1/3 cup rice vinegar
- 3 cups short-grain Japanese rice

For the Rolls
- 1 romaine lettuce heart
- Pickled ginger
- 20 asparagus spears
- Wasabi paste
- 10 nori sheets
- 1 plum tomato
- 1 small red onion
- 1 cucumber
- 1 avocado
- Sesame seeds

Method:
1. In a pressure cooker, mix the rice and 3 ¼ cup liquid and prepare according to the package recommendations.
2. In a small saucepan, mix the vinegar, salt, and 1 teaspoon sugar, mixing to absorb the sugar.
3. Fill a big wooden bowl halfway with cooked rice.
4. Soak your palms in water and spoon a pinch of rice onto the nori.

5. Range the rice uniformly up to the nori's edges by pressing it forward.
6. Sesame seeds may be sprinkled on top.
7. Get the veggies together. Cover with the loading.
8. Sushi rolls can be cut into 6 - 8 bits.
9. Serve with more miso and sticky rice.

8.3 California Sushi Rolls

Cooking Time: 1 hour
Serving Size: 64
Ingredients:
- 1 medium ripe avocado
- Reduced-sodium soy sauce
- 1 small cucumber
- 3 ounces imitation crabmeat
- 2 cups sushi rice
- Bamboo sushi mat
- 8 nori sheets
- 2 cups water
- 2 tablespoons sesame seeds
- 2 tablespoons black sesame seeds
- ¼ cup rice vinegar
- ½ teaspoon salt
- 2 tablespoons sugar

Method:
1. Merge rice and water in a big frying pan and set aside for thirty minutes.
2. Get the water to a boil. Cover and set aside for ten minutes.
3. In the meantime, whisk together the vinegar, syrup, and salts in a shallow saucepan until the sugar dissolves.
4. Drizzle the vinegar solution over the rice in a wide shallow dish.

5. Place aside the toasted and black sesame seeds on a tray.
6. Put ¾ cup rice on a piece of plastic wrap.
7. Place a tiny amount of cucumber, lobster, and avocado around 1-½ inches from the nori sheet's bottom side.
8. Roll up the rice mixture and place it on top of the filling.
9. Remove the mat from the sushi rolls and cover them with sesame seeds.
10. To make six rolls, repeat with the remaining components.
11. If required, top with soy sauce, miso, and herb slices.

8.4 Sushi Rice

Cooking Time: 25 minutes
Serving Size: 15
Ingredients:
- ¼ cup white sugar
- 1 teaspoon salt
- ½ cup rice vinegar
- 1 tablespoon vegetable oil
- 3 cups water
- 2 cups white rice

Method:
1. In a ramekin or strainer, wash the grain until the water flows clean.
2. In a small saucepan, mix the ingredients with the water.
3. Bring to the boil, then decrease to medium heat and simmer for 20 minutes, covered.
4. Water should be consumed, and the rice should be soft.
5. Allow cooling before you can handle it.

6. Mix the rice wine vinegar, oil, butter, and salt in a shallow saucepan.
7. Cook until the sugar has dissolved over medium-high heat.
8. Allow cooling before stirring into the boiled rice.
9. It will appear very moist as you spill this into the rice.
10. Continue to stir the rice as it condenses, and it may dry out.

8.5 Nigirizushi

Cooking Time: 30 minutes
Serving Size: 1
Ingredients:
- Nori; as needed
- Nikiri sauce
- Wasabi; as needed
- Sushi rice

Method:
1. Break the nori into pieces for nigirizushi that include a string of nori to tie the sushi intact.
2. Add a tiny knob of wasabi to the grain for nigirizushi that needs it between both the rice and the coating.
3. Place the topping of your choice on top of the rice noodles.
4. If nori is being used, coil one of the nori band ends tightly around the nigiri sushi coating, ensuring that it adheres to the rice and filling.
5. Use a small volume of spray, wet the other nori bands' end, and loop it around the topping, overlapping the other nori side.
6. The nori ends to hold together as a result of the warm water. Serve right away.

8.6 Mazesushi

Cooking Time: 50 minutes
Serving Size: 4
Ingredients:
For the Rice
- 2 tablespoons sugar
- 1 teaspoon salt
- 100 ml rice vinegar
- 320 grams Japanese rice

For the Vegetables
- 1 small carrot
- 200 grams enoki mushrooms
- ½ tablespoon sugar
- ½ tablespoon mirin
- 1 tablespoon Japanese soy sauce
- 45ml of dashi stock

For the Salmon
- Salt and black pepper, to season
- 1 tablespoon of sunflower oil
- 2 salmon fillets

For the Egg Crepes
- Juice of ½ lemon
- 1 -2 sheets toasted nori
- About ¼ teaspoon salt
- Sunflower oil
- 1 ½ tablespoons sugar
- 4 medium eggs

Method:
1. In a pressure cooker, add the water and prepare the rice.
2. In a shallow saucepan, mix the rice wine vinegar, salt, and seasoning and bring to a boil.
3. In a medium bowl, add the dashi box, sesame oil, sugar, and miso to a boil.

4. Cook, regularly mixing, until the vegetables and mushrooms are tender.
5. Powder the fish with black salt and pepper.
6. Add the oil and cook for five minutes on either side in a pan.
7. Allow the salmon to cool before removing the bones and flaking it.
8. Remove from the method.
9. Fold the liquor solution into the boiled rice with a light hand.
10. Combine the vegetables and mushrooms in a mixing bowl.
11. Add lemon juice and stir it in softly.
12. Create the crepes with the eggs.
13. To serve, layer the rice on sheets and top with the tuna, nori, and scallions.

8.7 Sushi Bake California Maki

Cooking Time: 40 minutes
Serving Size: 20 portions

Ingredients:

Sushi Rice

- 1 tablespoon sugar
- 1 teaspoon salt
- 3 tablespoon rice vinegar
- 4 cups freshly cooked rice

Furikake

- 1 teaspoon salt to taste
- 1 teaspoon sugar to taste
- ½ cup Korean roasted seaweed
- ½ cup sesame seeds

Creamy Topping

- Salt to taste
- 20 sheets Korean seaweed sheets
- ¼ cup Japanese mayonnaise
- 1 tablespoon Sriracha

- 2 cups Kani shredded
- 200 grams cream cheese
- 1 medium cucumber
- 1 big ripe mango

Method:
1. In a small container, whisk together the rice wine vinegar, spice, and sugar.
2. Heat it in the oven until the sugar and salt have fully dissolved.
3. Toss the properly prepared rice with the combination until it is uniformly spread.
4. Mix the cream cheese, Japanese mayo, and Sriracha in a mixing dish.
5. Insert the Kani, a third of the peach, and a third of the cucumber.
6. Make sure to save some of the mango and cucumber for further texture.
7. Season with salt to taste.
8. Place the sushi rice thinly in a rectangular pan and gently press it flat.
9. Spread a thin layer of Fukikake over the rice until it is fully coated.
10. Layer the creamy topping uniformly on top.
11. Cook at 200°C for fifteen minutes.

Chapter 9: Japanese Ramen Recipes

9.1 Japanese Ramen Noodle Soup

Cooking Time: 20 minutes
Serving Size: 4
Ingredients:
- 400g sliced cooked pork
- 2 teaspoon sesame oil
- 1 teaspoon white sugar
- 375g ramen noodles
- ½ teaspoon Chinese five-spice
- Pinch of chili powder
- 700ml chicken stock
- 1 teaspoon Worcestershire sauce
- Thumb-sized piece of ginger
- 4 tablespoon soy sauce
- 3 garlic cloves, halved

For the Garnish
- Sliced green spring onions
- Sprinkle of sesame seeds
- 4 boiled eggs
- 1 sheet dried nori
- 4 tablespoon sweetcorn
- 100g baby spinach

Method:
1. In a stockpot or big saucepan, combine chicken stock, garlic, sesame oil, Chinese five-spice, a finger slice of ginger, Worcestershire sauce, a pinch of chili flakes, and water.
2. Bring to the boil, then minimize heat to a simmer for five minutes.
3. Heat the ramen noodles according to the package directions.

4. Cook fried pork or chicken slices in sesame oil until lightly browned, then set aside.
5. Use four pans, separate the noodles.
6. A fifth of the beef, spinach, sweetcorn, and double-boiled egg halves are placed on top.
7. Split the stock among the pots, then top with nori sheets, fresh basil or parsley, and sesame seeds.
8. When serving, enable the vegetables to wilt somewhat.

9.2 Simple Homemade Chicken Ramen

Cooking Time: 1 hour
Serving Size: 2
Ingredients:
- 2 (3 oz.) packs ramen noodles
- Fresh jalapeño slices
- 2 large eggs
- ½ cup scallions
- 2 chicken breasts
- 1 oz. shitake mushrooms
- 1–2 teaspoon sea salt, to taste
- Kosher salt
- 2 tablespoon mirin
- 4 cups rich chicken stock
- Black pepper
- 3 teaspoon fresh garlic
- 3 tablespoon soy sauce
- 2 teaspoon sesame oil
- 2 teaspoon fresh ginger
- 1 tablespoon unsalted butter

Method:
1. Preheat oven to 375 degrees Fahrenheit.
2. Dress the chicken with salt and pepper.

3. In a big oven-safe pan, heat the oil over medium-high heat.
4. Cook the chicken with the skin cut side.
5. Roast for twenty minutes in the oven with the pan.
6. In a big pot, add the oil over a moderate flame until it shimmers.
7. Cook for a few minutes before the garlic and ginger is soft.
8. Mix in the soy sauce and mirin to mix.
9. Get the stocks to a boil, covered, before adding the dried mushrooms.
10. To make the soft-boiled whites, first cook the eggs in salted water.
11. Slice the green onion and jalapeno in the meantime.
12. Then use a sharp knife, cut the chicken into thin slices.
13. Transfer the ramen noodles to the hot water after the eggs have finished cooking.
14. Cook for three minutes, just until the noodles are tender, then split into two big bowls.
15. Mix the cut chicken and ramen broth in a large mixing bowl.
16. Small green onion, jalapeno, and a soft boiled egg go on edge. Serve right away.

9.3 Shoyu Ramen

Cooking Time: 1 hour
Serving Size: 6

Ingredients:
Kombu Dashi and Tare
- 2 tablespoon dry sake

- 1 tablespoon mirin
- ½ cup soy sauce
- 2 pieces kombu

Pork and Stock
- 1 1" piece ginger
- 2 carrots, peeled
- 1 head of garlic
- ¼ cup bonito flakes
- 1 lb. pork spareribs
- 2 bunches scallions
- 1½ lb. boneless pork shoulder
- 2 tablespoon vegetable oil
- 2 lb. chicken necks
- Kosher salt and black pepper

Ramen and Garnishes
- Six scallions, thinly sliced
- 3 toasted nori sheets
- 6 5-oz. packages ramen noodles
- ½ cup menma
- 3 large eggs

Method:

1. In a big mixing pot, mix Kombu and 4-quart jars of ice water for the dashi.
2. Cover and set aside for at least eight hours and up to twelve hours at ambient temperature.
3. In a shallow mug, mix the soy sauce, sake, and sesame oil; cover and cool.
4. Using salt and black pepper, spice the pork shoulder.
5. Pull it up and tie it at 2" stages with kitchen twine.
6. In a big heavy kettle, heat the oil over moderate flame.
7. Cook for 10–12 minutes, rotating once until the pork shoulder is brown all over.

8. Combine the meat, spareribs, green onions, carrots, cloves, ginger, and bonito flakes in a large mixing bowl.
9. Remove the Kombu from the dashi and discard it. Get the water to a boil.
10. Remove the pork shoulder from the stock and set it aside to cool.
11. Cover securely in cling film and place in the refrigerator before ready to use.
12. A large pot of water should be brought to a boil.
13. Continue adding the eggs one at a time and cook for seven minutes on low heat.
14. To avoid the eggs from frying, drain them and place them in a bowl of ice water to chill.
15. Remove the string from the pork and slice thinly; cover and put aside.
16. Ramen is ready to be served.

9.4 Rich and Creamy Tonkotsu Ramen Broth Recipe

Cooking Time: 12 to 18 hours
Serving Size: 6 to 8
Ingredients:
- 6 ounces whole mushrooms
- 1 pound slab pork fatback
- 2 whole leeks
- 12 garlic cloves
- One 3-inch knob ginger
- 2 dozen scallions
- 2 tablespoons vegetable oil
- 1 large onion, skin on
- 2 pounds chicken backs and carcasses
- 3 pounds pig trotters

Method:
1. Fill a big stockpot halfway with cold water and add the pork and chicken bones.
2. Bring a pot of water to a boil over medium temperature.
3. When the pot is boiling, gently smoke vegetable oil in a large cast-iron or nonstick pan over a high temperature.
4. Combine the onions, cloves, and ginger in a large mixing bowl.
5. Return the roasted tomatoes, leeks, spring onion whites, mushrooms, and meat fatback to the oven. Fill the container with cold water.
6. Heat over medium heat until the broth is decreased to around three quarts.
7. Cooked pork fatback should be finely chopped and whisked into the finished broth.
8. Dress broth with toppings of your choice before serving.

9.5 Japanese Duck Ramen Noodles

Cooking Time: 15-30 minutes
Serving Size: 4
Ingredients:
Duck
- 2 teaspoon Chinese 5-spice powder
- Salt
- 2 duck breast fillets

Broth
- 3-4 tablespoon soy sauce

- 300g egg noodles
- 4 spring onions
- 1 tablespoon sesame oil
- 1.2 liters chicken stock
- 2 fat cloves garlic
- 2-star anise
- 5cm knob grated ginger
- 2 whole chilies

Toppings
- 4 spring onions, sliced
- Sliced chilies
- ½ cup bean sprouts
- Handful fresh coriander
- 4 boiled eggs

Method:
1. Season duck skins with salts and Chinese 5-spice.
2. For five minutes, bake at the optimum temperature your oven can achieve.
3. Put down for ten minutes to recover. Before eating, slice the meat.
4. In a big kettle, combine all broth components except the noodles.
5. Bring to a boil, then reduce to low heat and cook for fifteen minutes.
6. Place the noodles in a warm bowl.
7. Pour the broth over it.
8. Sliced duck, poached egg, bean sprouts, basil, red onion, and chilies are served on top.

9.6 Instant Pot Ramen Recipe

Cooking Time: 25 minutes
Serving Size: 6
Ingredients:

- Black and white sesame
- Chili oil
- 2 tablespoons soy sauce
- 4 stalks scallion
- 3 packages of ramen noodles
- 8 oz. bok choy
- 1 lb. chicken tenders
- 2 cups water
- 4 eggs
- Salt
- 1 ½ tablespoon vegetable oil
- 4 cups chicken broth
- Ground black pepper

Method:
1. On all sides of the meat, sprinkle with salt and ground black pepper.
2. Switch the Instant Pot to Sauté stage.
3. Sear the poultry in an oven until both sides are golden brown.
4. Add chicken stock, water, and the green onions white bits.
5. Bring to a simmer and switch the pressure cooker to "Automatic" for ten minutes.
6. Make the ramen eggs in the meantime.
7. Switch the Instant Pot to Fast Release as it buzzes.
8. Switch on the Sauté function and add the poultry and ramen noodles as long as the soup starts to boil.
9. Then insert the bok choy and sesame oil. Toss the ramen about a little.
10. Cover the pot and switch off the Sauté mode.
11. The ramen noodles can be divided into four cups.
12. Serve the ramen right away.

9.7 Tonkotsu Ramen Recipe

Cooking Time: 16 hours 20 minutes
Serving Size: 8-10 bowls

Ingredients:

Tonkotsu Ramen

- 2-3 oz. enoki mushrooms
- Green onions
- 12 oz. ramen noodles
- 4 large eggs
- 8 cups tonkatsu pork broth

Chashu Pork Belly

- 2-3 cloves garlic
- 2 green onions
- ½ cup mirin
- ¼ cup sugar
- 2 lb. pork belly
- ½ cup sake
- ¼ cup soy sauce

Soy Bacon Tare

- 2 tablespoon sake
- 4 tablespoon Shiro miso
- ¼ cup soy sauce
- 2 tablespoon mirin
- 2 slices bacon

Miso Tare

- Pinch shichimi togarashi
- 1-2 teaspoon kosher salt
- ¼ cup sake
- ¼ cup mirin
- ½ cup Shiro miso

Method:

1. In a Ziploc container, mix the soy, rice, mirin, salt, cloves, and fresh basil.
2. Preheat the oven to 170°F and sous vide the meat for 10-11 hours.
3. Let the pork out of the Ziploc bag.
4. The container and marinade should be thrown out.
5. In a deep saucepan, mix all of the pulled pork components.
6. Simmer for about an hour at the lowest temperature.
7. If necessary, add a splash of chicken stock.
8. In a shallow saucepan, mix all of the miso tare components and cook on the lowest heat for about five minutes.
9. Get the eggs to a boil.
10. Simmer the ramen noodles in a large pot of water according to the package directions.
11. Heat the mushrooms in the same pot as the noodles.
12. Cook the chashu pork slowly.
13. Toss in the pasta. Add another 1½ cups tonkatsu soup to each bowl.

9.8 Tonkatsu Ramen Soup

Cooking Time: 15 minutes
Serving Size: 2

Ingredients:

- 1 green onion
- 1 teaspoon of sesame oil
- Water
- 1½ tablespoon of dashi stock
- 2 tablespoon of usukuchi soy sauce
- 1½ tablespoon of Weipa

Method:

1. Heat all of the condiments together in an oven.
2. Vegetable buds or green onion heads may be added.
3. Include an instant ramen bar.
4. Bring to a boil, and insert sesame oil.
5. Add one tablespoon each of condiments and sesame oil.
6. Heat for five minutes and serve right away.

Chapter 10: Most Famous Japanese Dishes

10.1 Sesame-Ginger and Cucumber Soba Noodles

Cooking Time: 28 minutes
Serving Size: 6
Ingredients:
- 2 tablespoons sesame seeds
- Sea salt, to taste
- Pinch red pepper flakes
- ⅓ to ½ cup water
- 1 teaspoon sesame oil
- Handful fresh cilantro
- 8 ounces soba noodles
- 1 tablespoon white miso
- 2 teaspoons tamari
- 2 small English cucumbers
- 2 tablespoons rice vinegar
- 1 tablespoon fresh ginger
- ⅓ cup tahini
- 1 bunch scallions

Method:
1. Heat the soba pasta to al dente, as per box instructions, in a big pot of salted water.
2. Cut the cucumber into thin, skinny strips with a paring knife or, better still, a julienne slicer.
3. Combine the tahini, garlic powder, ginger, sesame oil, veggie broth sauce, sesame seed, coriander, and red pepper flakes in a shallow dish.
4. In a large mixing bowl, mix the soba noodles with the sesame-ginger sauce.

5. Toss in the cabbage strips, green onions, red pepper, and, if needed, more coriander. Serve right away.

10.2 Omurice

Cooking Time: 25 minutes
Serving Size: 2
  Ingredients:
  For Ketchup Fried Rice
- 1 tablespoon ketchup
- 1 teaspoon soy sauce
- ⅛ teaspoon kosher salt
- 2 servings cooked Japanese rice
- ½ onion
- 1 tablespoon olive oil
- ½ cup mixed vegetables
- 1 chicken thighs

  For Omelet
- 2 tablespoon olive oil
- 6 tablespoon sharp cheddar cheese
- 2 tablespoon milk
- 2 large egg

Method:
1. Collect all of the necessary ingredients.
2. Thinly slice the onion.
3. In a nonstick skillet, add the oil and cook the onion once softened.
4. Heat until the meat is no longer yellow.
5. Sprinkle with salt before adding the sautéed veggies.
6. Split the rice into tiny chunks and add it to the pot.
7. Use a spatula to distribute the ketchup and soy sauce uniformly.

8. Clean the pan after removing the fried rice from a tray.
9. In a shallow pan, whisk together one egg and one tablespoon dairy.
10. In a moderate pan, heat one tablespoon olive oil.
11. Drop the beaten eggs into the pan until it is heated and tilt it to cover the pan's bottom.
12. Sprinkle the ketchup on top as a finishing touch.

10.3 Kitsune Udon

Cooking Time: 20 minutes
Serving Size: 2
Ingredients:
For Soup Broth
- 1 tablespoon usukuchi soy sauce
- ½ teaspoon kosher salt
- 1 tablespoon mirin
- 1 teaspoon sugar
- 2 ¼ cups dashi

For Kitsune Udon
- 4 slices narutomaki
- Shichimi Togarashi
- 4 inari age
- 1 green onion
- 2 servings of udon noodles

For Homemade Dashi
- 1 kombu
- 1 ½ cups katsuobushi
- 2 ½ cups water

Method:

1. In a measurement cup, combine the Kombu and 2 ½ cup water for at least thirty minutes.
2. Rinse for three hours or upwards to half a day if you have the room.
3. In a saucepan, combine the Kombu and the water.
4. Over moderate pressure, slowly bring to a simmer.
5. Reduce the heat to low and allow the dashi to simmer for fifteen seconds before turning off the heat.
6. Take the dashi, miso, one teaspoon salt, sesame oil, and sugar to a boil in a saucepan.
7. For the udon noodles, bring a big pot of water to the stove.
8. In a pot of boiling water, steam the dried udon noodles for ten minutes.
9. In serving pots, combine udon noodles and spicy broth.

10.4 Unagi no Kabayaki

Cooking Time: 40 minutes
Serving Size: 4
Ingredients:
- 800g eel

Pickles
- 1 garlic clove
- 2 tablespoon apple cider vinegar
- ½ cabbage
- 1 small knob of ginger
- 5 teaspoon salt
- 1 apple
- 1 carrot
- 1 teaspoon rice flour

Kabayaki Sauce
- 120g white sugar
- 350ml Japanese soy sauce

- 100ml sake
- 120g raw sugar
- 300ml mirin
- 1 eel bone

Method:
1. In a frying pan, combine the salt, corn starch, and liters of water for the olives.
2. Put to a boil, stirring constantly.
3. Place the carrot, apple, cabbage, spice, and garlic in a large mixing bowl.
4. Shake softly to incorporate the apple cider vinegar.
5. Heat the eel bones over coal until golden for the kabayaki seasoning.
6. To cook off the liquor, carry the mirin and sake to boiling in a frying pan for about ten seconds.
7. Hot water should be poured over the eel shell.
8. Barbecue for 5-10 minutes, meat side down rotating often.
9. Brush the kabayaki sauce only on the crispy texture for 4-5 minutes or until finely glazed.
10.   Take the steak from the grill and cut it into small strips.
11.   Serve with boiled vegetables as a side dish.

10.5 Japanese Pork Cutlet Rice Bowl Katsudon

Cooking Time: 40 minutes
Serving Size: 2

Ingredients:
- Chopped green onion
- 2 bowls of cooked rice

For The Katsu
- 1 tablespoon milk
- 100g panko breadcrumbs
- 4 tablespoon plain flour
- 1 large egg
- Pinch of salt and pepper
- Vegetable oil
- 2 boneless pork chops

Katsudon
- 1 teaspoon tsuyu sauce
- 2 eggs
- 2 tablespoon soy sauce
- 1 tablespoon sugar
- 2 tablespoon sake
- 2 tablespoon mirin
- 100ml water
- 1 large white onion

Method:
1. To begin, cook rice in a pressure cooker with liquid.
2. Season all sides of the pork chop with salt and black pepper.
3. To begin, flour both sides of the beef.
4. Soak them in a mixture of egg and milk.
5. Position the coated chicken breasts in the oil cautiously and bake for four minutes on either side or until lightly browned.
6. Discharge the excess oil by placing the katsu on a wire shelf.
7. Slice each onion into thinly sliced and fried for a minute or so in a pan over medium heat.
8. Combine the rest of the ingredients and stir well.

9. When the onions are loosening, break two eggs into a mixing bowl and whisk them together.
10. In the same pan, insert the katsu and the egg.
11. Allow for 1-2 minutes of cooking time.
12. Serve with chopped green onion or your favorite greens as a garnish.

10.6 Edamame with Soy and Sesame Sauce

Cooking Time: 5 minutes
Serving Size: 2

Ingredients:
- 1 teaspoon soy sauce
- Salt and pepper to taste
- 2 tablespoons toasted sesame oil
- 150 grams edamame in pods

Method:
1. Bring 3-4 minutes to boil edamame.
2. Drain and rinse with a towel in the cool spray.
3. Transfer sesame oil to a skillet over medium temperature.
4. Transfer the edamame pods to the sweet, nearly smoking oil and fry for around 2-3 minutes.
5. Stir in the soy sauce until it has completely evaporated.
6. Dress with salt and pepper to taste.
7. Serve right away or keep it in the fridge until later.

10.7 Chawanmushi

Cooking Time: 30 minutes
Serving Size: 4

Ingredients:
- Pinch of salt
- Tsuyu
- 1 teaspoon soy sauce
- 1 teaspoon sugar
- 3 eggs
- 8 slices kamaboko steamed fish cake
- 1 teaspoon cooking sake
- 4 large cooked prawns

- 4 shiitake mushrooms
- 240ml dashi stock

Method:
1. Begin by gently whisking the eggs in a mixing cup, making sure they do not froth up.
2. Combine the dashi storage, sesame oil, boiling sake, sugar, and salt in a separate dish.
3. To get a decent blend, add this mixture to the eggs when stirring constantly.
4. Pour the water from the shiitake mushrooms, strip the roots, and cut in half.
5. A shallow bowl or cup for each places two cut shiitake pieces, one big prawn, and double slices of kamaboko.
6. Filled the cups up to the brim with the beaten egg.

10.8 Curry Rice

Cooking Time: 30 minutes
Serving Size: 6
Ingredients:
- Fukushinduke
- Worcestershire sauce
- Pinch of salt and pepper
- 2 cups water
- 1 2/3 cups Uncooked rice
- ¼ cup grated apple
- 1 tablespoon honey
- ½ a large packet of Curry Roux
- 1 tablespoon olive oil
- 2 cloves of garlic
- 9 oz. protein
- 1 large potato
- 1 carrot

- 1 brown onion

Method:
1. Begin cooking the rice.
2. Set aside the beef, which has been cut into bite-size portions.
3. Set down the potatoes, carrots, and onion after peeling and cutting them into big bite-size sections.
4. In a medium-sized kettle, heat the olive oil and add the garlic.
5. Heat the onion after the garlic has become fragrant.
6. Cook the meat until it turns a whitish brown, then add the carrot, cabbage, and onion and whisk with a wooden skewer.
7. Combine the sugar, butter, and diced apple in a mixing bowl.
8. To moisten the sauce, reduce the heat to low and bring to boil.
9. In a shallow dish, place the fried plain rice and spill the curry over it.
10. If desired, garnish with Fukushinduke and Rakkyo.

Conclusion

Without a doubt, Japan has become one of the world's great food countries. New seasonal harvest and gentle preparation are the key components of Japanese cuisine. Japanese cuisine has exploded into the culinary scene. It's no surprise that Japanese cuisine is so common, given its mastery of flavors and delicate balance of sweet and savory. Japanese and Japanese-inspired foods can be found worldwide, even in the local kitchen, mainly seafood and ramen. Water is also at the heart of Japanese food, with dashi made from Kombu (kelp) and bonito particles in water serving as the basis for all Japanese sauces. The essence of Japanese cuisine is new, seasonal flavors cooked simply in water. As a result, it carries the "healthy" label well. To get the delicious Japanese food tastes back, you don't need to become a master chef. The only way of learning about Japanese cuisine is to try it. Read the Japanese cookbook and enjoy yourself while tasting everything Japan has to offer.

Vegetarian Japanese Cookbook

Japanese Food Made Simple with Over 77 Easy Recipes for Amazing Veggie Dishes

Adele Tyler

The trademarks that are used are without any consent, and the publication of the trademark is without permission or backing by the trademark owner. All trademarks and brands within this book are for clarifying purposes only and are the owned by the owners themselves, not affiliated with this document.

Introduction

With a boundless array of local and regional foods, Japanese cuisine promises an assortment of gastronomic pleasures. There is a wide selection of dishes and ethnic specializations of Japanese food. Japan is broken into different regional areas, each of which has formed its distinctive culinary traditions. Consequently, as they pass from place to place, travelers may experience a varied range of national foods.

Japanese food has taken the horticultural environment by storm. With its distinctive skill of flavorings and a sensitive mixture of salty and sweet, it is no wonder Japanese ingredients are so common. From ramen to sushi, dishes influenced by Japanese and Japanese could be seen anywhere, such as your country's restaurants! To take home the magnificent ingredients of Japanese food, you do not need to be a professional chef.

It can be tough to be a vegan in Japan, but it can also be very satisfying with some preparation and advance scheduling. Rice, pasta, seaweed, vegetables, soy goods, and mushrooms make extensive Japanese food use. But no food is more embedded in fish than Japan's, as a country comprising many large Island nations. Seafood is Japan's main common cuisine, and ingredients extracted from fish are now almost inevitable. All of this provides the reputation of Japanese food as one of the most plant-based of all foods and one of the most vegetarian at the same time. It is too hard to request a vegan meal consistently at a traditional Japanese restaurant that you definitely might as well not make an effort. The diet gets irritatingly close to being completely vegan in certain ways.

Fish is simple enough to resist, but ingredients dependent on seafood are not. In Japanese cuisine, a spice compound called dashi typically made mainly from fish flakes turns up anywhere.

They place it in sauces, fried rice, spices for eating, serving, and many other tasty foods. The umami taste is provided by Dashi, which cannot be easily copied with the other common Japanese additives. There are vegetarian varieties of dashi, of course, but you are only likely to discover it easily. Pork is not a common part of Japanese cuisine, but through Japan's similarity to China, it is become a common Japanese food in recent years. It is typically placed into Gyoza fritters, and tiny pork spice quantities are also used in Japanese veggie dishes. In the whole of their meals, a lot often Japanese chefs typically put meat or fish seasoning.

"Vegetarian Japanese Cookbook" has all vegetarian recipes. It has four chapters with a short introduction to Japanese cuisine and some historical facts. Chapter two, three, and four discuss Japanese breakfasts, snacks, lunch, dinner, soups, and a few famous vegetarian recipes from Japanese cuisine. Learn 77 recipes of delicious and easy Japanese vegetarians from this book and prepare your vegan meals.

Chapter 1: A Brief Introduction to Japanese Food

Each food is named "Gohan." by the Japanese. For instance, breakfast is called "asa-Gohan." In traditional Japanese dishes, a cup of boiled rice is also included and may be a component of dinner, breakfast, or lunch. The side dishes are known as okazu and are eaten with broth and rice. A component of Japanese food is rice. It is also popular to eat rice cakes (mochi). They vary from savory to sweet and have many different methods, from grilled to boil. With heavy effects from both Korea and China, Japanese cuisine has been around for more than centuries. And it's only been several decades before all the results of what is now recognized as Japanese cuisine has begun to exist. Currently, the four seasons and climate also have a significant influence on Japanese food. Most frequently, fish and veggies are consumed. Although the food may sound almost ordinary to some western people; tastiness, appearance, and combination of flavors are of utmost importance.

1.1 History and Facts of Japanese Cuisine

Japanese food has been affected by other civilizations' food practices, but it has adapted and modified to establish its distinctive form of preparing food behaviors. About 300 B.C., China was the very first foreign intervention in Japan. When they learned to raise rice from the Japanese. China was also responsible for using utensils and soybean curd production (tofu), and soy sauce.A further significant effect on Japanese food was the Buddhist faith, one of the two main Japanese historical beliefs. In the 700s A.D., the emergence of Buddhism resulted in a prohibition on consuming meat.

As a consequence of that prohibition, the famous dish, sushi, came into being. Cooking patterns became easier in the 19th century. Tiny amounts were prepared with a wide range of vegan (non - meat) ingredients, with five major cooking methods. Five color classes (green, yellow, white, red, and black-purple) and six flavors were broken into all products (salty, sour, bitter, hot, sweet, and delicate). The Japanese prefer to use this preparation method.

Trade with the rest of the countries started introducing foreign ideas to Japan starting in the early 13th century. The Dutch brought bread, cabbage, and sweet potatoes. The Spanish established tempura. During the Meiji Era, the meat went to Japan after a prohibition of even more than thousands of years. During the late 20th century, Modern items, such as coffee, bread, and frozen yogurt, became popular. The adoption of time-saving cooking techniques has become another Westernization. This includes the automatic slow cooker, frozen foods such as pot noodles, broth, and quick pickling blends for quick miso (fermented bean powder). The Japanese, though, are also committed to their rituals of classic cuisine.

Rice arrived from Korea, wheat and soybean came from China and a crucial Japanese cuisine component. In Britain, yogurt and other dairy products have struggled to enjoy the same success as In Japan. Between both the eighth and fifteenth generations, the only Japanese dairy material documented in history was made. It was also just for pulling carts or plowing fields that cattle were bred. It was, until quite lately, a long-forgotten tradition to use them for beef or even dairy.

The absence of beef products also reduced the use of spices. From the seventh century, peppers and garlic were recognized and were introduced either through China or indirectly from Asian Countries, and slight garlic was also produced. But these herbs were mostly used for the manufacture of drugs and cosmetics.

Fish was an important replacement in the lack of beef, and, as both an island nation, this food source was plentiful and inspired many of the world's most common dishes before modern distribution methods were adopted; however, the complexity of storing and shipping fresh aquatic fish reduced consumption in inland areas because, previously, aquatic fish are widely consumed.

Japanese food is associated with better food and has a deep relationship with the region's long-expected lifespan. One of the key factors behind all this is 'ichijyusansa' that applies to a meal composed of brown rice and broth, the main dish of fish or meat, and a fresh salad of vegetables or seaweed, all slightly flavored to display the components' natural flavors.

Wasabi is among the globe's most challenging ingredients to produce, and that is why the crop is so pricey. Many wasabi in cafes are usually horseradish combined with food dye processing for this purpose. True wasabi has a more herbal taste than the artificial type, but it lacks its punch for about fifteen minutes after being diced.

1.2 Japanese Food Cooking Methods

There are different techniques for preparing Japanese food. Some of these are:

Yakiniku

Yakiniku describes a Japanese method of cooking bite-sized parts of vegetables and meat on a plate grill.

A variety of dishes prepared using the same method may also be referred to. Yakiniku has Korean roots and was influenced by the popular Korean foods, but yakiniku meat is typically not sautéed before barbecuing. Unrefined, finely cut meat and veggies are typically taken to the plate and fried by individuals.

Yakiniku's most common meat involves pork, beef, poultry, and a selection of shellfish. On the other hand, various spices and sauces are typically served - from sesame oil and miso sauce to pesto with garlic oil.

Teppanyaki

A Japanese method of cooking several ingredients on an iron ring is Teppanyaki. Its name derives from two phrases: "teppan," or plates of iron, and "yaki", means grilled or roasted. Teppanyaki applies to the above method of preparing several dishes. Many of the most common teppanyaki forms are sausages, fish, diced veggies, rice, and bread foods such as yakisoba rice noodles. The iron plates are also put in front of the clients in Modern kitchens to see the chef's function.

Teriyaki

Teriyaki is a Japanese cooking method in which, after being brined in red sauce, the components are lightly seared, fried, or grilled, composed of mirin, soy sauce, and syrup. A fusion of two things is teriyaki: Teri, which meant luster, and yaki, indicating to broil or grill. Teriyaki plates, accomplished by teriyaki sauce, are distinguished by their polished and glinting overall aspect. Food historians say that teriyaki, together with various other dishes containing fried or grilled beef, was first developed in the seventeenth century by Japanese cooks.

Dry-Frying

Karaage, often termed dry-frying, is a Japanese cooking method in which numerous food items are first gently wrapped, then deep-fried, in arrowroot flour.

Arrowroot flour maintains the organic moisture content of fried foods and creates a crisp outer layer. Still, it is also possible to use other protective layer flavors such as tapioca, rice flour, or cornmeal as an option.

Karaage could be used to fry different meats and vegetables. Still, it is most often correlated with poultry. It includes a specific method named tatsutaage, wherein chicken parts are first salted in a combination of sake, sesame oil, and soy sauce, which is then gently coated and deep-fried with arrowroot flour.

Chapter 2: Japanese Vegetarian Breakfast and Snack

2.1 Japanese Breakfasts Recipes

Japanese Rice Balls

Cooking Time: 45 minutes

Serving Size: 30

Ingredients:

- Salt
- Sushi rice 1 cup

Lime-Avocado

- ¼ avocado
- 1 lime, juice + zest

Bell Pepper

- ½ teaspoon fresh ginger
- Salt, pepper
- 1 roasted bell pepper
- 1 tablespoon peanut butter

Edamame-Sesame

- 2 tablespoon black sesame seeds
- ¼ cup of edamame

Cilantro-Scallion

- 2 chopped scallion
- 2 tablespoon chopped cilantro

Miso-Walnut

- 2 tablespoon chopped walnut
- 1 tablespoon miso paste

To Decorate

- Sesame seeds
- ¼ avocado, thinly sliced
- 1 sheet of nori

Method:

1. Wash rice in a plastic container. Add rice and one bowl of water to a pan.

2. Bring to a simmer over medium temperature and minimize to low flame.

3. Slow cooker and boil the rice for approximately fifteen minutes just till the water is completely incorporated. Let the rice cool a little bit.

4. In the meantime, get your fillings ready.

5. Mix the bell pepper, peanut butter, spice, seasoning with a mixing bowl, and then transfer to a dish.

6. Combine miso and nuts; sesame seeds and edamame; coriander and spring onion; avocado, lemon zest, and juice.

7. Split the rice between all the cups and combine the fillings around.

8. Wet your palms, scoop out some rice, and carefully form the rice into a triangular or ball.

9. Use a piece of nori or diced avocado to cover Onigiri, or spread them over a tray of sesame seeds.

Japanese Breakfast Porridge Bowl

Cooking Time: 10 minutes

Serving Size: 1

Ingredients:

- 20g of firm
- Water for desired consistency
- 1 tablespoon nutritional yeast
- ¼ of a small avocado
- 20g round brown rice (dry)
- 1 nori sheet, shredded
- 1 teaspoon miso paste
- ½ cup chopped leek
- 20g rolled oats

To Garnish

- Sesame seeds
- Paprika powder

Method:

1. Begin by draining brown rice. Wash and clean.

2. Place the rolled oats in a shallow saucepan in the morning before preparing the porridge, then add only enough hot water to fill them. Just put aside.

3. You could either rip the nori papers with your palms or cut them with knives.

4. Then, cook the soaked rice and the sliced leek in a room temperature water frying pan till the rice is ready, about ten minutes.

5. Turn the heating off. Then, blend in the soaking rolled oats and insert the appropriate boiling water.

6. Then, combine some liquid with miso paste and switch things up with ripped nori paper and nutritional yeast into the mixture.

7. Again, when necessary, add a little water.

Tamagoyaki Scramble

Cooking Time: 3 minutes

Serving Size: 1

Ingredients:

- ¼ teaspoon black salt
- pepper to taste
- 2 teaspoon sugar (10g)
- ⅛ teaspoon baking powder
- ½ teaspoon kombu dashi
- 2 teaspoon mirin (10g)
- 1 sheet yuba
- 3 tablespoon liquid of choice
- 1 teaspoon soy sauce
- ¼ cup silken tofu (60g)

Garnish

- Scallions
- Sesame seeds

- Kizami nori
- Soy sauce

Optional

- 1 tablespoon vegan kewpie mayo
- Pinch of turmeric
- 2 teaspoon nutritional yeast (8g)

Method:

1. Moisturize in warm water for 3-5 minutes, dry yuba.
2. Rip the yuba into smaller parts, about around the size of a fist.
3. Mix soy milk, silken tofu, mirin, soy sauce, rice, dashi, sugar, and baking powder thoroughly together.
4. This is going to be the eggy mixture, which shuffles as well.
5. Over medium-high heat, warm a bowl, and add oils or vegetarian butter.
6. Add the silken tofu and put the yuba stuff on top. Before handling it, let it cook for around two minutes.
7. Use spoons or a spatula until the sides start to look fried, then force the sides into the center.
8. Lower the heat and simmer for another thirty seconds, moving the egg mixture to the right texture every few minutes.
9. Squeeze the black salt on edge using your fingertips.

10.   Take it out of the oven and eat on the sides or over pasta.

Miso Soup with Tofu, Wakame Seaweed

Cooking Time: 15 minutes

Serving Size: 2

Ingredients:

- ½ cup chopped green onion
- ¼ cup firm tofu
- 3-4 tablespoon white miso paste
- ½ cup chopped green chard
- 1 sheet nori
- 4 cups vegetable broth

Method:

1. In a small saucepan, put the vegetable broth and take it to a low boil.
2. Meanwhile, place the miso in a shallow saucepan (starting from the smaller end of that scale), add that little warm water, and swirl until soft.
3. When applied to the broth later, this would guarantee that it does not bind. Just put aside.
4. Transfer chard (or other leaves of your choice), spring onions, and tofu to the liquid (insert at the end of a meal, if silken is used) and cook for five minutes.
5. Insert nori, now, and mix. Add the miso solution, detach from the flame, and whisk to blend.

6. When desired, try and add further miso or a touch of kosher salt. Serve it warm.

Macrobiotic Pearled Barley Ojiya

Cooking Time: 35 minutes

Serving Size: 3

Ingredients:

For the Pearled Barley

- A pinch of sea salt
- 1 cup pearled barley

For the Ojiya

- ½-1 tablespoon barley miso
- Scallions, for garnish
- 2 tablespoons diced celery
- 1 tablespoon sliced leek
- 1 cup cooked pearled barley
- 2 tablespoons diced carrots
- ¼ cup diced onion

Method:

1. Place the pearled barley in a frying pan with soaking water and kosher salt.

2. Bring to the boil, seal, minimize to medium heat, and steam for 45-50 minutes.

3. Take from the fire and leave to steam for ten minutes or sit. Balance the cooked grains softly.

4. In a small saucepan, put cooked pearled grain and 2/3 of a cup of hot water and bring to the boil.

5. Add the carrots, onions, celery, and leek. Cover and cook for ten minutes, or until the vegetables are tender.

6. Add a little liquid if you like a soupier texture and boil until it becomes soft.

7. Decrease the heat to a low level and insert a small liquid volume to melt the miso in a shallow bowl.

8. To the bowl, insert miso. If required, change the taste. For five more minutes, continue simmering.

9. Serve hot with your choice of dressings.

Tamago Kake Gohan

Cooking Time: 50 minutes

Serving Size: 2

Ingredients:

- 1 scallion, finely chopped
- Sesame seeds, for sprinkling
- Extra-virgin olive oil
- 2 eggs
- Splashes of tamari
- 3 cups cooked brown rice

Optional Toppings

- Avocado slices
- Roasted broccoli
- Microgreens
- Splash of rice vinegar

- Thinly sliced nori

- Japanese pickles

- Extra egg yolks

Method:

1. Squeeze out two cups of fried brown rice.

2. Put 1 egg per cup alongside splatters of tamari when the rice is boiling, and mix rapidly so that the egg heats softly while the rice covers, giving the rice a creamy texture.

3. Cover each cup with spring onions, pumpkin seeds, and the extra toppings you want. Serve on the surface with miso for flavor.

Egg-and-Miso Breakfast Soup

Cooking Time: 20 minutes

Serving Size: 1

Ingredients:

- Chopped scallions

- Coarse salt and ground pepper

- 1 large egg

- 1 cup baby spinach

- 2 tablespoons white miso

Method:

1. In a skillet, put 1 ½ cups of water on the stove. Mix until it disperses fully in miso.

2. Put the eggs softly in a tiny bag, then slip them softly into the simmering liquid.

3. Cook for about two minutes before the whites are just fixed, and the yolk is still watery.

4. Add spinach and steam for about two minutes, until softened.

5. Spray with spring onions and add salt and black pepper to spice.

Japanese Natto

Cooking Time: 5 minutes

Serving Size: 1

Ingredients:

- 1 teaspoon soy sauce
- 3 shiso leaves
- Steamed Rice
- 1 tablespoon Katsuobushi bonito flakes
- Japanese yellow mustard
- 1 tablespoon green onions
- 1 package Natto

Method:

1. Combine all the components, excluding the shiso and steamed rice.

2. Mix very well until it is dense.

3. Place the rice around and line it with Shiso.

Tofu Hiyayakko

Cooking Time: 10 minutes

Serving Size: 1

Ingredients:

- 1 pinch bonito shavings
- 1 pinch toasted sesame seeds
- 1 ½ teaspoon fresh ginger root
- ¼ teaspoon green onion
- 1 tablespoon soy sauce
- ½ teaspoon water
- ¼ (12 ounces) package silken tofu
- ½ teaspoon dashi granules
- 1 teaspoon white sugar

Method:

1. In a shallow bowl, blend the sugar, dashi granules, soy sauce, and water when the sugar is dissolved.
2. On a small dish, put the tofu and cover it with green onion, ginger, and bonito granules.
3. Sprinkle on top of the soy combination and scatter with sesame seeds.

Vegan Japanese Souffle Pancakes

Cooking Time: 20 minutes

Serving Size: 2

Ingredients:

Dry Ingredients

- ¼ teaspoon baking soda
- Pinch of salt
- 1 tablespoon sugar
- 1 teaspoon baking powder
- 80g all-purpose flour

Wet Ingredients

- 2 teaspoons oil
- 1 teaspoon vanilla extract
- 1 tablespoon apple cider vinegar
- 80ml soy milk

Method:

1. Lubricate the appropriately with oil or vegetarian butter when you're using ring molds.
2. Mix the flour mixture very well in a pan.
3. Shift the flour mixture on the one hand and insert the apple cider vinegar, vanilla extract, plant-based milk, and oil.
4. Slowly pour together all the products until no dry patches remain. Do not spill over.
5. Over moderate fire, heat a wide skillet.
6. Transfer a thin film of oil to the rim. Turn the heat down to moderate when the oil is hot.
7. Position the molds of the ring so that among them, there seems to be some room.
8. Twice, the batter is spooned under one mold, then the other.

9. Now scoop the batter into two large piles when you're not using a mold. Use a lid to protect the pot and let it heat for ten minutes.

10. The surfaces of the cakes should never be shiny for more than ten minutes.

11. They must have some wrinkles on the horizon, and that they should appear dry on the bottom. Switch the pancakes using a spatula.

12. However, place the bowl once more and cook for the next three minutes before the pancakes are cooked fully.

13. Remove and expose the bowl from the flame.

14. The cores of the pancakes should be softly squeezed to monitor for doneness.

15. They can quickly pop back up. On a tray, cut the cakes.

16. Slide a slim spatula or the end of a blade around to loosen the cakes by cutting the ring mold.

17. Serve with a vegetarian oil or a coconut whip and golden syrup instantly.

Japanese Vegan Pancakes Dorayaki with Red Bean Filling

Cooking Time: 20 minutes

Serving Size: 2

Ingredients:

- Vegetable oil
- ½ cup red bean paste
- 2 tablespoon mirin or maple syrup
- ¼ teaspoon soy sauce
- ½ cup sifted cake flour
- 2 teaspoon baking powder
- ⅓ cup soy milk
- 2 tablespoon powdered sugar

Method:

1. In a large cup, mix the flour, icing sugar, and cornstarch.

2. Add the maple syrup, soy milk, and soy sauce to some other dish.

3. To form a delicious mixture, drop the dried mixture into the wet one, and mix.

4. It is not meant to be so dense, but this should be small enough just to pour. For ten minutes, let everything sit.

5. In a non-stick pan or pot, pour that small amount of oil and warm it over moderate flame.

6. To disperse the oil equally, use a towel. You just want the slightest amount to help shade the pancakes but not adhere to them.

7. Reduce heat to medium, and dump about two tablespoons of the batter in as ideal the round as you can find on the non-stick plate.

8. You need all of them to be approximately the same number.

9. For around two minutes, heat on the first hand, bubbles might rise on edge, and the sides will cook very easily.

10. For around one more minute, turn and heat on the other hand.

11. Enable your cakes to chill for several minutes, then add a dollop of Anko, the bean paste, to each of them.

12. To make the Dorayaki, cover it with a croissant and stack it all together.

13. Serve with a swirl of icing sugar or cream cheese or diced strawberries with almond.

2.2 Japanese Snacks Recipes

Vegetarian Ramen

Cooking Time: 1 hour

Serving Size: 4

Ingredients:

- 4 baby bok choy
- 4 5-oz. packages ramen noodles
- 3 tablespoon unsalted butter
- 1 tablespoon soy sauce
- 4 garlic cloves
- 8 dried shiitake mushrooms
- 1 piece dried kombu
- ¼ cup vegetable oil
- 1 2" piece ginger
- 2 tablespoon tomato paste
- 1 tablespoon black sesame seeds
- Kosher salt
- 4 scallions
- 1 tablespoon. gochugaru

Method:

1. Cook the garlic and ¼ cup of the oil in a medium saucepan over medium heat, frequently whisking, until the garlic is translucent, around four minutes.

2. Mix in the sesame seeds and roast until the garlic is nicely browned and crisp, turning periodically, for about two minutes.

3. To a small pan, move the mixture and mix in the gochugaru; sprinkle with salt.

4. Place aside the garlic oil. Clean the pot away and set it aside.

5. Cut green onion with dark green pieces and small pieces; put down for serving.

6. Chop the green and white pieces coarsely.

7. Heat the remaining two tablespoons of oil to moderate in the preserved pot.

8. Cook the sliced green onion and ginger for about four minutes, stirring regularly, until the scallions are crispy in patches.

9. Insert the tomato sauce and simmer for about two minutes, stirring regularly, before it appears to adhere to the sides of the pan and blackens gradually.

10. Insert the Kombu and mushroom, then whisk in five cups of cold water.

11. Bring to a boil, then remove from heat and leave to rest for about ten minutes while the mushrooms weaken. Drop the Kombu and dispose of it.

12. Move the solids to a mixer using a rubber spatula.

13. To mix, add a spoonful or two of liquid and purée until creamy.

14. Stir the purée in the bowl back into the liquid and bring it to a boil over medium-high heat.

15. Add oil a slice at a time, until introducing more, whisking to mix with each addition.

16. Add soy sauce and stir; sprinkle with salt. Lower the heat and stay warm until ready for serving.

17.   In the meantime, put it to a boil with a big pot of water. Insert bok choy and cook for about two minutes until it is greenish and soft.

18.   Move Bok Choy to a table that used a rubber spatula. Bring the mixture to a boil and prepare the noodles as instructed by the box. Drain between bowls and split.

19.   Spoon the liquid over the pasta to eat, then finish with bok choy and the preserved garlic oil. If needed, finish with nori, eggs, and coriander.

Creamy Miso Pasta with Tofu and Asparagus

Cooking Time: 20 minutes

Serving Size: 2

Ingredients:

For Pasta

- ¼ teaspoon kosher
- Freshly ground black pepper
- 1 firm fried tofu
- 1 tablespoon olive oil
- 4 oz. asparagus

For Cooking Spaghetti

- 2 teaspoon miso
- 1 teaspoon soy sauce
- Soy milk sauce
- ½ cup unsweetened soy milk
- 7 oz. spaghetti

- 1 ½ tablespoon sea salt

Method:

1. Collect all the components.

2. Mix a half cup of soy milk, two teaspoons of miso, and one teaspoon of soy sauce in a mixing cup and blend it.

3. Approximately twice the sum of these components if you want to turn it into "soup noodles."

4. With a clean cloth, cover the tofu and extract any humidity. Split into small pieces of tofu.

5. Cut off the asparagus edges and cut them into small slices horizontally.

6. Begin to boil four quarters of water in a big saucepan. Put one and a half tablespoon of salt and pasta until boiling.

7. Mix to ensure that the pasta does not stay together.

8. Over moderate flame, warm the olive oil in a deep pan fryer.

9. Insert the cubes of tofu and simmer until they are seasoned and hot with oil.

10. Insert asparagus, then add salt to the seasoning.

11. To the bowl, transfer the soy flour mixture and reduce the heat to a moderate flame.

12. Set aside four tablespoons of pasta water and transfer to the cooking pot.

13. If the "soup noodles" are made, put three more tablespoons of pasta water.

14. This point should finish your pasta.

15.   Use a large spoon to grab the pasta (or you can rinse them easily in the sink) and add them to the plate.

16.   Reduce the heat to moderate and mix all of the pasta to combine.

17.   If required, flavor and add the salt.

18.   For separate pots, serve the spaghetti. If you like a hit of seasoning, scatter with Shichimi Togarashi.

Vegetable Gyoza

Cooking Time: 2 hours

Serving Size: 80

Ingredients:

For Gyoza Filling

- 1 clove garlic
- 2 tablespoon potato starch
- 2 green onions
- 1 knob ginger
- 12 oz. extra firm tofu
- 5 oz. king oyster mushrooms
- 2 oz. carrot
- 3 oz. onion
- 2 oz. shiitake mushrooms
- 5 oz. cabbage
- 1 teaspoon kosher salt
- 3.5 oz. red cabbage

For Dipping Sauce

- ⅛ teaspoon la-yu
- 1 tablespoon soy sauce
- 1 tablespoon rice vinegar

For Gyoza Filling Seasonings

- 1 teaspoon kosher salt
- ⅛ teaspoon white pepper powder
- 1 tablespoon miso
- 2 teaspoon sesame oil
- 2 tablespoon soy sauce

For Frying Gyoza

- ¼ cup water
- 1 teaspoon sesame oil (roasted)
- 1 tablespoon oil

For Gyoza

- Water
- 80 Gyoza wrapper

Method:

1. Collect all the components. Place a washcloth over the tofu and put it on a tray.

2. Place another layer on top of the tofu, then, with a large weight or two, force the tofu hard for about one hour.

3. Put two tablespoons of soy sauce, two teaspoons of sesame oil, one tablespoon of miso, and ⅛ teaspoon of white pepper into a small pan.

4. Mix and put down altogether.

5. Cut into tiny bits the julienned cabbage.

6. For red cabbage, keep repeating the same thing. In a cup, place the diced cabbage and add the salt.

7. Use your hands to clean the cabbage and carefully remove it before it absorbs water.

8. Break the carrot into tiles and slice the onions into tiny bits.

9. Break the spring onions into pieces that are white and green.

10. Remove the king oyster mushrooms at the lower part, slice them into pieces, and slim them.

11. Dispose of the shiitake mushroom head, slice it into pieces, and then slim it.

12. Add the two types of mushroom, carrots, onion, and spring onions into a big cup.

13. Then continue cooking, and add garlic, which is minced.

14. Chop the ginger and grind it. Insert one teaspoon of rubbed ginger.

15. Try squeezing the water out of the cabbage and apply all of the components to the cup.

16. The tofu chunks are then sliced into pieces and then squares.

17. In the pan, add the tofu blocks and the Gyoza Filled Spice combination and blend it.

18. When the seasoning blends are covered with the products, insert the potato starch.

19.   Spray any potato starch on a sheet or plate of paper towels.

20.   Cover the wrapping over the lining in part and press it with your fingertips in the middle.

21.   Over medium pressure, steam the oil in a pan non-stick deep fryer. When it is hot in the skillet, put the Gyoza.

22.   Cook for about three minutes before the Gyoza tops turn light golden. To the bowl, add ¼ cup of hot water.

23.   Close the Gyoza instantly with a cap and heat for about three minutes or before much of the water disappears.

24.   To disappear any water left, remove the cap. Transfer 1 teaspoon of sesame oil to the frying pan.

25.   Bring the sauce components together for the dipping sauce. Serve hot.

Vegan Poke Bowl

Cooking Time: 20 minutes

Serving Size: 2

Ingredients:

For Pan-Fried Tofu

- ½ tablespoon rice vinegar
- 1 teaspoon chili paste (Sambal Oelek)

- 1 tablespoon sesame oil (roasted)
- 3 tablespoon soy sauce
- 1 block fried firm tofu
- ⅛ onion

For Vegan Poke Bowl

- ½ teaspoon sesame seeds
- ½ teaspoon white sesame seeds
- 2 cups cooked brown rice
- 2 tablespoon shelled edamame
- 1 carrot
- ¼ English cucumber
- ½ avocado
- 1 lime
- ½ watermelon radish
- 2 green onions
- ⅛ red cabbage

Method:

1. Collect all the components.
2. Start cooking the veggies next if you want to make delicious tofu, and come back to this phase later. Instead of that, cut the white onion finely.
3. Open and extract all moisture from the tofu packet.

4. Break the tofu, about twelve bits, into bite-sized bits.

5. Then warm the sesame oil across moderate heat in a large cooking pan and add the large onion.

6. Sauté once oil covers the onions. Insert the blocks of tofu next.

7. Insert Rice Vinegar, soy sauce, and sambal oelek as soon as the tofu is covered with oil.

8. Decrease the oven temperature and cover the liquid with the tofu.

9. Switch off the fire and, when the tofu is well-coated with the liquid, extract it from the stove.

10. Break the carrot into specific shapes and then slice it into pieces of julienne.

11. Take the skin of the cucumber, leave a portion unpeeled and slice it into small strips.

12. Chop the radish from the watermelon and slice it into small pieces.

13. Break the green cabbage's tough heart and slice finely.

14. Trim the spring onions horizontally into thin slice.

15. Chop the avocado softly and cut it into ½ inch strips.

16. Break the avocado into pieces, then. To keep it from overcooking, split the lime in two and pour the juice over the avocado.

17. In two big pots, prepare the fried brown rice.

18. First, put the weighty vegetables, such as avocado, fry tofu, and red cabbage.

19. The remainder of the components is then added.

20.   Spray the end with sesame seeds and spring onions.

Japanese Mitarashi Dango

Cooking Time: 15 minutes

Serving Size: 2

Ingredients:
- 4 tablespoon filtered water
- ½ cup sweet rice flour (mochiko)

Sauce
- 2 teaspoon mirin
- 1 teaspoon arrowroot starch
- 1 tablespoon soy sauce
- 1 tablespoon coconut sugar
- 3 tablespoon filtered water

Other
- Wood skewers
- Toasted nori sheet

Method:
1. Over moderate flame, ready a pot of boiling water, and bring it to a boil when cooking your Dango flour.
2. Mix the water and sweet rice flour in a measuring dish.
3. Proceed with a spoon and mix to blend, then begin using your hands to work the flour.

4. You want a strong dough that doesn't cling to your side but keeps to itself and is feasible.

5. Do it by gently washing your hands and rubbing again if you need to apply more water.

6. Not adding so much water is necessary, so begin with less and add as more required.

7. Break into 6 bits and shape into little balls until you have a functional dough.

8. Drop softly into the pot while the water boils and steam for about five minutes, and until the Dango is floating and is baked all the time through.

9. When cooking your gravy, rinse and move to a bowl of ice water.

10. Mix all the arrowroot flour in a shallow bowl with a drop of cold water to create sludge.

11. First, mix gluten-free soy sauce, coconut sugar, water, and mirin in a shallow skillet over medium heat.

12. Stir to mix, add the slurry of arrowroot flour and begin stirring until the mixture thickens.

13. Turn off the heat until the sauce thickens, then put it aside.

14. Drain the Dango again, though, and skewer three bits with each piece.

15. Glaze to the palate of your sweet soy glaze and eat!

Chapter 3: Vegetarian Japanese Lunch and Dinner

3.1 Japanese Lunch Recipes

Vegetarian Okonomiyaki

Cooking Time: 30 minutes

Serving Size: 2

Ingredients:

Vegetarian Okonomiyaki

- 2 spring onions, thinly sliced
- 1 tablespoon oil
- 120 grams shredded green cabbage
- 1 small carrot, grated
- ½ teaspoon pureed ginger
- Black pepper
- 4 eggs
- 1 tablespoon soy sauce
- 80 grams plain flour

To Serve

- Chopped spring onions
- Sesame seeds
- Sriracha
- Mayonnaise or salad cream

Method:

1. In a blending pan, beat the eggs and then insert the flour.

2. Mix to shape the mixture for the pancake.

3. Include the pureed ginger and soy sauce, lots of black pepper, then insert the carrot, cabbage, and spring onions that are finely chopped. To blend, combine well.

4. In a deep fryer, warm a bit of oil, and teaspoon in ¼ of the pancake combination.

5. Heat for several minutes over medium-high heat, till the underneath is nicely browned, then gently flip a spoon over the pancake and cook for a few more minutes, till cooked thoroughly.

6. Repeat to make four pancakes in sum with the leftover pancake combination.

7. With salad sauce, Sriracha cut green onions, and sesame, eat the vegan okonomiyaki with that as well.

Japanese Soba Noodles

Cooking Time: 20 minutes

Serving Size: 6

Ingredients:

- ½ cup green onions minced
- 3 tablespoons sesame seeds
- 1 tablespoon canola oil
- 2 cups green onions
- 10 ounces Soba Buckwheat Noodles

- ¼ teaspoon ground black pepper
- 1 tablespoon sugar
- 1/3 cup Double Fermented Soy Sauce
- 3 tablespoons toasted sesame oil
- 2 tablespoons rice vinegar

Method:

1. Carry a big pot of water on the stove and make soup the soba pasta for five minutes or even just until soft, occasionally mixing so the pasta does not tangle.

2. Wash in a colander and pat dry under ice water, dumping to erase the starch.

3. When the pasta is frying, sweep the sesame oil, soy sauce, sugar rice vinegar, and black pepper together in such a small dish. And put aside.

4. Over medium flame, heat a large skillet.

5. Insert the canola oil and flame the sliced spring onions until they glitter.

6. Heat for fifteen seconds or until aromatic, mixing.

7. Insert the sesame and soy mixture and reheat for thirty seconds.

8. Put the pasta and toss till the pasta is warmed through.

9. Insert the leftover minced spring onions and a quarter of the seeds.

10. Garnish with the residual seeds and eat at low temperatures or hotter.

Green Bean Shiraae (Mashed Tofu Salad with Green Bean)

Cooking Time: 30 minutes

Serving Size: 2

Ingredients:

- 9 oz. green beans
- 7 oz. silken tofu

Seasonings

- 1 teaspoon soy sauce
- ⅛ teaspoon kosher salt
- 1 tablespoon sugar
- 2 teaspoon miso

4 tablespoon white sesame seeds

Method:

1. Collect all the products.
2. Hold it in an enclosed jar and add water before it fills the tofu to hold the remaining tofu.
3. Leave it in the fridge (start changing the water daily) and use it for a few periods.
4. You would not want to drain water from the tofu fully, but some humidity must be removed so that the coating does not become too wet.
5. Place paper towels around the tofu.
6. On a sheet or pan, place the sealed tofu.
7. On top of the tofu, place another plate or tray and carry a massive item on top to allow drainage. Place thirty minutes free.
8. Put to a boil a huge pot of boiling water. Blow the sides of the green beans apart.
9. Boil up the crisp-tender green beans.

10.   Well, rinse and put aside.

11.   Break the green beans into small bits horizontally.

12.   Pour in the soy sauce and mix them around. For later, put aside.

13.   In a cooking pot, roast the sesame seeds, constantly tossing the wok, till they are aromatic and starting to pop. Switch to a Japanese mortar.

14.   With a pestle, crush seeds.

15.   Add the miso and honey.

16.   Mix well before the crushed sesame seeds are mixed into the sugars and miso.

17.   Withdraw the tofu from the clean cloth.

18.   Use the hands to split it into bits and transfer it to the sesame seed combination.

19.   Tasting the tofu and seasoning with salts to taste is essential. It is not meant to be dull.

20.   Put all together till perfect.

21.   Be careful to first clean off some surplus soy sauce from the beans.

22.   Just the seasoning will weaken the fluid from the soy sauce.

23.   The cooked green beans are then added to the tofu seasoning. Mix well.

24.   When mixed, you can cool for thirty minutes in the fridge before eating or serve instantly.

Soy-Glazed Eggplant Donburi

Cooking Time: 20 minutes

Serving Size: 2

Ingredients:

- 4 tablespoon neutral-flavored oil
- ½ teaspoon white sesame seeds
- 1 knob ginger
- 2 tablespoon potato starch
- 10 shiso leaves
- 7 oz. Japanese eggplant

Seasonings

- 2 tablespoon soy sauce
- 4 tablespoon mirin

Method:

1. Collect all the components.
2. Round the eggplant into ¼-inch pieces and insert iodine.
3. Put aside for fifteen minutes and put a hand towel to clean off the humidity.
4. Wash the shiso leaf and use a hand towel to clear. Dispose of the ends.
5. Fold and slice the shiso ends into slices or chiffonade.
6. Slice off the skin of the ginger and grind the spice. You require one teaspoon of ginger.
7. Add two tablespoons of potato starch to a serving dish and cover the eggplant pieces on both edges loosely.
8. Heat 2 tablespoons of oil over medium-high heat in a cooking pot.

9. Add the eggplant pieces to a thin layer when the pan is heated.

10. Cook till it is nicely browned on the back end, around three minutes.

11. Do not hit the eggplants before then to obtain a good sear.

12. Whenever the lowest surface is perfectly fried, sprinkle on top of the remaining oil (2 tablespoons) and turn the eggplant slices for around 3-4 minutes to fry the other half.

13. Turn down the heat to moderate flame until this portion is cooked until lightly browned; insert mirin, soy sauce, and mashed ginger.

14. Take it down to a boil and spill the sauce a couple of times over the eggplant.

15. If the sauce has thickened too easily, put one tablespoon of water to soften it a little. Whenever the eggplant is very well with the sauce, withdraw it from the flame.

16. In a donburi dish, serve boiled rice (slightly larger than a sushi roll) and rain with some sauce.

17. Spray with seeds and decorate with shiso leaves. Instantly serve.

Tofu Katsu with Spicy Sweet-Sour Sauce

Cooking Time: 15 minutes

Serving Size: 24

Ingredients:

- Sunflower or canola oil
- Sweet chili sauce, to serve
- ½ cup Aquafaba
- ½-1 cup breadcrumbs
- 200 grams firm tofu
- 2 tablespoon plain flour
- Soy sauce

Method:

1. First, to eliminate the extra humidity and digest flavors faster, we have to 'push' the tofu.

2. Cover a few paper towels with the tofu, put it on a plate, and load it off with something hard.

3. Shift it to a fresh one until the paper towel gets wet. Repeat till the hand towel remains almost clean.

4. When the tofu is pounded, split the cube in half and finish with two layers that are fifty percent thinner.

5. Break any block into 12 bits. In a big, shallow cup, add some soy sauce and dump all the tofu pieces into it.

6. Pour ample soy sauce so that the tofu is at least half immersed.

7. Left it for thirty minutes to marinate, then turn over the tofu bits and keep for the next 30 minutes in soy sauce.

8. Combine multiple large cups, one of flour, the other about chickpea brine, and the last of cornmeal.

9. Cover each square of the tofu in chickpea brine, and in the flour, and after that in the breadcrumbs.

10. To create an even coverage on both sides, ensure you push each square's surface into the powder and cornflour well.

11. In a small deep fryer, pour 1 cm of butter and warm it gradually.

12. Drop a pair of breadcrumbs in to try it. It can cook if the oil sizzles as the breadcrumbs touch the ground.

13. Optionally, the heat of the oil can be measured-it can exceed around 175° C.

14. Push few more bits of tofu into the butter. However, the pan is not congested.

15. Cook them for around three minutes on each part (once this side becomes nicely translucent), and instead, use BBQ tweezers, switch them over.

16. If the first mixture is ready, scatter the tofu to wipe extra fat on a few paper towels and begin cooking another round.

17. Go on until you get all the tofu cooked. Enjoy it with a piece of warm chili sauce right now.

(Takikomi Gohan) Japanese Shiitake and Vegetable Rice

Cooking Time: 2 hours 30 minutes

Serving Size: 6

Ingredients:

- 2 scallions, thinly sliced

- ¼ cup frozen peas
- 6 ounces shiitake mushrooms
- ½ cup diced carrot
- 1 ½ cups short-grain brown rice
- 2 tablespoons reduced-sodium tamari
- Pinch of salt
- 2 tablespoons mirin
- 2 ½ cups Dashi Stock

Method:

1. In a medium skillet, place the rice and bring water to fill 2 inches.
2. To release the ground starch, squirt with your fingertips.
3. Drain boiling liquid off and repeat it two to three times, just until the liquid is almost clean.
4. In a sieve, spill the rice and leave to drain for five minutes.
5. Move the sieve a couple of times, then bring the rice back to the plate.
6. Insert mirin, dashi, salt, and tamari. Let it stay for thirty minutes.
7. Over moderate flame, take the solution to a lively boil, stirring regularly.
8. To sustain a low boil, reduce the flame, continue cooking for thirty minutes.

9. Place on top of the mushroom, carrots, and spring onion whites, continue cooking till the rice and veggies are soft, about fifteen more minutes.

10. Take it out of the flame and let it stay for ten minutes.

11. Over the tip, sprinkle the peas instead of filler the rice and blend with the lentils.

12. Wrap and then let stand for about ten minutes, till the peas are cooled. Before eating, whisk in the spring onion greens.

Vegetarian Katsu Curry

Cooking Time: 15 minutes

Serving Size: 2

Ingredients:

- 1 cup frozen stir fry vegetables
- Cooked rice
- 2 vegetarian schnitzels
- 1 block of Golden Curry

Method:

1. As advised, prepare the schnitzels or cutlets.
2. Break and set it aside into pieces.
3. Steam a pan and cook the veggies that are frozen.
4. To loosen the curry cube, insert the Golden Curry square, ½ cup of hot water, and mix.
5. Transfer a little extra water if the sauce gets too heavy.
6. Transfer the warm rice to a container to eat and put the bits of schnitzel on board.

7. Fill with the veggies and gravy and eat immediately.

Teriyaki Mushroom Bowls

Cooking Time: 45 minutes

Serving Size: 4

Ingredients:

- 2 tablespoon sesame seeds
- 2-3 scallions, sliced thinly
- 1 teaspoon red chili flakes
- 1 lb. broccolini, about 12 stalks
- 1 cup dry brown rice
- 2 garlic cloves, finely minced
- 2 teaspoon ginger, minced
- 6 Portobello mushrooms
- 1 tablespoon white miso paste
- 1 tablespoon brown sugar
- 3 tablespoon soy sauce
- 2 tablespoon rice vinegar
- 3 tablespoon sesame oil

Method:

1. Heat the flame to 425 degrees F.
2. Slice the mushrooms and cover them with 1 tablespoon of sesame oil.
3. Switch to a cookie dish and bake until the mushroom is soft and the liquid flows for twenty minutes, rotating halfway across.

4. Cook rice as per the instructions in the box.

5. In the meantime, in a small shallow saucepan, mix the brown sugar, rice vinegar, soy sauce, ginger, garlic, and chili powder.

6. Heat till the sugar dissolves, and the paste gets thicker into a coating, stirring regularly.

7. To smooth it out, if you moisten this too much, put in 1 tablespoon of water.

8. Shave the woody edges off the broccolini and sprinkle on a cookie dish with the leftover two tablespoons of sesame oil and salt season.

9. Pull them from the cooker until the mushroom is baked.

10. With both the teriyaki coating, coat all parts of the mushroom, and the red cabbage.

11. Put the broccolini and mushroom back in the oven for ten minutes before the broccolini is the saddle, and the mushrooms are caramelized.

12. Spray with sesame oil and clear everything from the cooker.

13. For a side dish, serve broccoli and mushroom over rice and finish with spring onions.

Spicy Tofu Bento Bowl

Cooking Time: 30 minutes

Serving Size: 6

Ingredients:

- 2 tablespoon sesame seeds
- 2-3 scallions, sliced thinly
- 1 teaspoon red chili flakes
- 1 lb. broccolini, about 12 stalks

- 2 garlic cloves, finely minced
- 2 teaspoon ginger, minced
- 1 tablespoon white miso paste
- 1 tablespoon brown sugar
- 1 cup dry brown or white rice
- 3 tablespoon soy sauce
- 2 tablespoon rice vinegar
- 3 tablespoon sesame oil
- 6 Portobello mushrooms

Method:

1. In a cup, combine the sesame oil, chili-garlic sauce, and soy sauce.

2. Over medium-high heat, warm a pan. Soak the tofu in a soy sauce combination; boil for ten minutes, or until golden brown. Let it for ten minutes to warm.

3. Transfer the leftover chili combination to the spring onions, cream, and lime juice. Toss on the tofu.

4. In a cup, combine the soy sauce, lime juice, spice, and chili-garlic sauce.

5. Add rice in bowls for dining. Top of the Greens.

6. Trim carrot stripes with a cheese grater over the end.

7. Place the tofu, celery, and carrot on top. Slather with sesame seeds; eat with a combination of soya sauce.

3.2 Japanese Dinner Recipes

Japanese Rice Balls with Avocado Filling and Sweet Potato

Cooking Time: 1 hour

Serving Size: 4

Ingredients:

- 1 teaspoon toasted sesame oil
- ½ avocado
- ½ teaspoon salt
- ½ – 1 small sweet potato
- 2 tablespoon rice wine vinegar
- 1 tablespoon sugar
- 3 cups water
- ¼ cup sesame seeds
- 1 ½ cup brown sushi rice

Teriyaki Sauce

- 2 tablespoons sugar
- 1 tablespoon rice wine vinegar
- 5 tablespoons soy sauce
- 5 tablespoons mirin
- Vegetable oil for frying

Method:

1. Begin by doing the rice cleaning.
2. Quantify the rice into the pan and wash it with cool water several times till the water no longer

looks murky and begins to appear clean. Drain some rice.

3. Use ice water to coat the rice, put the pot on the flame, and protect it with a cover. Switch the heat off when the water heats.

4. Offer it a stirring and allow the water to consume the rice.

5. The rice must be weak after thirty minutes. Drain all water in bulk.

6. Place the sugar, vinegar, and salt together in a shallow bowl and stir the sauce over the hot rice.

7. Insert the sesame seeds and completely combine them. At ambient temperature, just let rice settle.

8. The sweet potato is sliced and sliced into small strips.

9. In a vessel, steam the pieces until tender. Also, you should roast them.

10. Slice the avocado and chop it.

11. Strip a large mixing bowl with films from the kitchen and drop around one tablespoon of cooled rice in it.

12. Push on the firm sheet of rice. Take one piece (you will need to make it simpler) of sweet potato, dunk it in red sauce and place this over rice.

13. Placed a piece of avocado on each of the sweet potatoes as well.

14. With certain rice, surround the stuffing and push it into a standardized ball.

15. Take the Onigiri with cooking film from the bowl and form the palms with the rice ball. Remove the film.

16.   For the remainder of the rice and covering components, repeat.

17.   Preheat the frying pan and pour some oil over it.

18.   Fry Onigiri over medium temperature until crisp and well caramelized, three minutes per hand. Serve with teriyaki sauce instantly.

19.   Integrate the soya sauce, vinegar, mirin, and sugar in a shallow saucepan.

20.   Bring it to the boil with the gravy. Blend the corn starch with liquid in a tiny cup.

21.   Steadily dump the corn starch combination into the sauce when continuously stirring it.

22.   Continue cooking until you have caramelized the sauce. Switch the heat off over the pan.

Lightly Fried Japanese Vegetables

Cooking Time: 20 minutes

Serving Size: 2

Ingredients:

- Sea salt
- Toasted sesame seeds
- ¼ white cabbage, julienned
- 2 teaspoons mirin
- Sesame oil
- 1 tablespoon rice wine vinegar
- 1 tablespoon tamari

- 2 carrots, julienned
- 1 small red bell pepper
- 1 small white onion
- 4 spring onions, chopped
- 1 zucchini, thinly sliced

Method:

1. Over a high flame, warm up a big wok.
2. Insert the sesame oil and transfer the veggies until it is close to the combustion mark.
3. Let them stay in a wok until half of the wok is dark on one edge.
4. Mix the tamari, vinegar, and mirin of rice wine.
5. When stirring, spray the combination over the veggies to offer them some humidity.
6. To ensure they are always crisp, cook the veggies for two minutes.
7. If required, sprinkle them with kosher salt, put them on serving plates, and marinade them with toasted pine nuts.

Savory Mushroom and Vegetable Ramen Soup

Cooking Time: 40 minutes

Serving Size: 2

Ingredients:

- Salt, to taste
- Red chili flakes (optional)
- Juice from 1 lime
- Olive oil
- 6 ounces ramen noodles
- 2 cloves of garlic, diced
- 1 small shallot, diced
- 4 cups mushroom broth
- 1 cup baby kale
- ¼ cup grated rainbow carrots
- 1 cup broccoli
- ½ cup beech mushrooms
- 1 cup shiitake mushrooms

Method:

1. Heat the broccoli, then preheat the pan on the stove over hot water and insert some olive oil.

2. Transfer to the pot two minced garlic cloves and a tiny shallot, let them boil once transparent, and afterward insert diced mushrooms.

3. Heat the mushrooms, cloves, and shallot for several minutes, then insert a tamari dash and little kale sauces and simmer until the kale begins to ripen.

4. The broccoli must be soft by then, so take it out of the flame and put it aside.

5. Take four cups of liquid to boil in a pot and add the pasta to prepare the ramen.

6. You can begin to split gradually, with a spoon, you can move them apart while cooking quicker.

7. Transfer the soup and pasta to a container with kale, mushrooms, and broccoli whenever the pasta is heated.

8. On edge, grind some rainbow vegetables, red chili powder, a combination of natural seaweed particles, a sprinkle of pepper, and one lemon juice.

Somen Noodles with Nori Dressing

Cooking Time: 1 hour

Serving Size: 2

Ingredients:

For the Noodles

- 2 packages of somen noodles

For the Seaweed Dressing

- ½ teaspoon sesame oil

- A pinch of salt

- 2-3 tablespoons sesame seeds

- 1 teaspoon sugar

- 2 sheets of nori

For Toppings

- Nuts

- Carrots, matchsticks

- 2-3 scallions, sliced thin

- Sesame seeds

- Kimchi or shredded cabbage

- Sliced cucumbers

For the Sauce

- 2 tablespoons sesame oil
- A splash of maple syrup
- 2-3 tablespoons rice vinegar
- 2-3 tablespoons tamarin

Method:

1. Cook the pasta as per the directions provided in the box.
2. Mix all the components for the sauces and set them aside.
3. Combine and set it aside from the components for the seaweed coating.
4. Break the pasta into two cups.
5. Place over the sauces and marinade with the toppings you like. Just serve.

Tofu Yasai Don: Japanese Tofu Rice Bowl

Cooking Time: 2 hours

Serving Size: 4

Ingredients:

- 4 green onions, sliced
- 4 teaspoons white sesame seeds
- 3 rehydrated Shiitake mushrooms

- 6-8 cups steamed Japanese rice
- 2/3 cup mirin
- 1 tablespoon fresh ginger juice
- 1 14-ounce block extra firm tofu
- 2 cups kombu Shiitake dashi
- 2/3 cup reduced-sodium tamari
- 4 ounces frozen, shelled edamame
- 2 slender carrots, peeled
- 1 medium Japanese sweet potato
- 1 slender burdock root

Method:

1. Wash the tofu and wipe it off with a hand towel.
2. Cover in a plastic wrap sheet and afterward cover in an aluminum sheet.
3. Refrigerate in the fridge for 24 hours. In the oven, melt.
4. Do not unpack tofu, but put it in a jar, sealed, as the liquid can leak.
5. It can take one to two nights to melt.
6. Once the tofu has thawed full, unscrew it and rinse off the excess moisture, then put it on a serving platter filled with many sheets of clean cloth.
7. Put on top some more sheets of the towel and then place it on the edge of a work surface.

8. With something like many food containers or a magazine, load the chopping board back and then let the tofu push for at least thirty minutes.

9. Break it into thin pieces until the tofu has been pounded, then put it aside.

10. Unpack it and brush off the excess moisture until the tofu has defrosted entirely, then put it on a serving platter filled with many sheets of clean cloth.

11. Put on top some more sheets of the towel, then place on each of that a work surface.

12. Use anything like multiple boxes of beans or a notebook to force the work surface back and let the tofu push for at least thirty minutes.

13. Break it into thin pieces until the tofu has been pounded, then put it aside.

14. Place the edamame, chilled and camped, in a jar, and fill it with liquid. Over moderate flame, carry the mixture to a boil, then extract the water and drain. Place back the defrosted edamame.

15. Use the end of a paring knife, scrape off from the outside coating of the burdock core, and slice it.

16. Begin at the heavier side and slice it lengthwise, with the blade at a 45° angle, about half-inch from the bottom.

17. Push the burdock core to you, flip approximately 1/3, and cut once more, helping to keep the knife figuring at the same 45 ° F viewpoint.

18. Continue to cut that way, varying your cuts' width and angles if required to create tiny pieces. Use the same tool, cut the sliced vegetables.

19.   Lengthwise, split the stripped Japanese zucchini in the quarter, then lengthwise, split each quarter in the quarter again.

20.   Break each quarter lengthways into ½-inch thinly sliced.

21.   In a small saucepan, mix the dashi, mirin, low sodium tamari, and spice extract. Brought to a gentle simmer over medium-high heat.

22.   Insert the burdock root, Japanese sweet potato, tofu, carrots, and bits of mushroom and boil until all the veggies are soft, uncovered.

23.   To sustain a steady simmer while you steam the veggies, reduce heat as required.

24.   Insert the edamame and bake for an extra minute, enabling the frying pan to heat it and consume the flavors.

25.   Place 1 and a half cups of warm rice into personal donburi baskets or big, shallow broth bowls to fit the rice bowls.

26.   The vegetables and tofu represent the rice. Spoon over each cup with a few teaspoons of frying liquid.

27.   Marinade and serve instantly with finely diced spring onion and toasted pumpkin seeds.

Chapter 4: Japanese Vegetarian Famous Recipes

4.1 Japanese Soup Recipes

Japanese Vegan Udon Noodle Soup

Cooking Time: 25 minutes

Serving Size: 4

Ingredients:

For the Broth

- Salt
- Pepper
- 2 tablespoons mushroom sauce
- ½ teaspoon chili paste
- 2 tablespoons rice vinegar
- ¼ cup soy sauce
- 4 cups vegetable broth
- 1 pinch sugar
- 2 pieces ginger

For Assembling

- ¼ cup cilantro (chopped)
- ½ cup peanuts
- 4 medium green onions
- 1 pound udon noodles

For the Chinese Broccoli

- 2 tablespoons sesame oil

- 1 pound Chinese broccoli
- ½ tablespoon ginger
- 2 cloves garlic
- 1 tablespoon peanut oil

Method:

1. Collect components.
2. Mix the veggie broth or vegan chicken stock with spice, rice vinegar, sugar, mushroom sauce, soy sauce, and chili paste in a small saucepan.
3. To mix, swirl to get to a boil. Turn down the heat and let it boil to a simmer.
4. Enable at least ten minutes for the liquid to boil.
5. Take from the stock, the bits of spice and dispose of them. With pepper and salt, dress gently.
6. Warm the sunflower oil in a different medium saucepan and insert minced garlic, ginger, and sesame oil.
7. For two or three minutes, let that be citrusy and add the minced Chinese kale.
8. Sauté for several moments, till the broccoli is just soft and the color is light green.
9. Cover and set it aside from the fire.
10. Put a portion of pasta in each, preparing individual cups, top it with the Chinese kale packed, a healthy portion of soup, some chopped spring onions, minced cilantro, and unsalted almonds.

Vegan Nabe (Hot Pot with Miso)

Cooking Time: 40 minutes

Serving Size: 4

Ingredients:

- 4 cups water
- Salt, to taste
- 2 pieces of kombu
- 4 Shiitake Mushrooms
- 1 handful Enoki mushrooms
- ½ Napa cabbage
- 1 handful Mizuna greens
- 2 tablespoon white miso paste
- 1 leek, sliced
- 1 dried chili pepper
- 1 tablespoon soy sauce
- 1 turnip, sliced thinly
- 1 small carrot, sliced

Method:

1. Add the water, shiitake mushrooms, leeks, kombu, turnip, carrot, chili pepper, and soy sauce to the pot.

2. For thirty minutes, carry to a light boil.

3. Meanwhile, in a small container, insert the miso and then pour a few cups of water once it becomes a dense sauce texture.

4. This would make the blending of the broth simpler.

5. Switch off the heating after thirty minutes.

6. If required, mix in the miso paste and salts and insert the mizuna, cabbage, and enoki mushroom.

7. Instantly serve.

15-Minute Miso Soup with Greens and Tofu

Cooking Time: 15 minutes

Serving Size: 2

Ingredients:

- ½ cup chopped green onion
- ¼ cup firm tofu
- 3-4 tablespoon yellow miso paste
- ½ cup chopped green chard
- 1 sheet nori
- 4 cups vegetable broth

Method:

1. In a small mixing bowl, put the vegetable broth and take it to a low boil.

2. Meanwhile, place the miso in a shallow saucepan (beginning from the smaller end of that scale), add a little more warm water, and swirl until soft.

3. When transferred to the broth later, this would guarantee that it does not clump. Just put aside.

4. Transfer chard (or other vegetables of your selection), spring onions, and tofu to the liquid

(insert at the end of the process, if silken is used) and cook for five minutes.

5. Insert nori, next, and mix. Add the miso solution, detach from the flame, and whisk to blend.

6. When desired, try and add additional miso or a touch of kosher salt.

7. Serve it warm. It is better when clean.

Kenchin Vegetable Soup

Cooking Time: 30 minutes

Serving Size: 4

Ingredients:

- 1 tablespoon sesame oil
- ½ tablespoon oil
- 500ml boiling water
- 1 stem shallot
- ½ pack firm tofu
- 50g carrot
- 100g taro
- 125g konnyaku (½ pack)
- 50g shimeji mushrooms
- 70g daikon

Dashi Broth

- 2 tablespoon sake
- A pinch of salt
- 2 tablespoon soy sauce
- 800ml dashi stock

Method:

1. Use a paper towel to seal the tofu and position it on a flipped baking sheet.

2. On the tofu, put a tiny work surface or a jar with weights in it.

3. Leave it for another thirty minutes. Before processing the veggies, make this move.

4. Lengthwise, split konnyaku into several identical pieces.

5. Then cut each patch to 5millimeters wide parallel to the first slice.

6. A pot of hot water over the bits of konnyaku, wash.

7. Halve the squeezed tofu horizontally onto the cutting surface.

8. Cut the three sides of tofu half down the middle, then cut diagonal to the second piece to 1.5cm thick.

9. In a frying pan, add sesame seed and butter and cook over a medium temperature.

10. Place all the veggies in the pot, excluding the shallots and tofu, and cook till the vegetable parts are covered in oil.

11. Insert the tofu, then the components from Dashi Broth.

12. Set a cover on and simmer for about five minutes just until the veggies are heated through. Bring it to boiling.

13. Pull the scum from periodically while frying.

14. Transfer the shallots to the skillet, stir for fifteen seconds or so, and then switch the heat off.

15. While warm, eat.

Hearty Vegetable Miso Soup

Cooking Time: 30 minutes

Serving Size: 4

Ingredients:

- 2 potatoes
- 1-2 carrots (peeled)
- 1 onion
- 5-6 mushrooms
- 2 tablespoon peanut oil
- 4 tablespoon miso paste
- 4 cups water

Method:

1. Split herbs, no bigger than ¾-inch, into small bites.

2. Sauté the vegetables in a broth sauté pan in heated oil till they become transparent; then insert the other veggies and sauté for another three minutes.

3. Add the water and cook till all veggies are tender; minimize heat to medium and insert miso paste to boil.

4. Bring to a boil and add diced leeks or cut spring onions to flavor.

4.2 Famous Japanese Recipes

Yasai Itame

Cooking Time: 30 minutes

Serving Size: 4

Ingredients:

- 1 tablespoon neutral-flavored oil
- 3.5 oz. bean sprouts
- 1 clove garlic
- 1 knob ginger
- 6.5 oz. thinly sliced pork
- ¼ cabbage
- ½ carrot
- ¼ onion
- 10 snow peas

For Pork Marinade

- 1 teaspoon sake
- 1 teaspoon soy sauce

For Seasonings

- Freshly ground black pepper
- 2 teaspoon sesame oil
- 1 teaspoon soy sauce
- ½ teaspoon kosher salt
- 1 teaspoon oyster sauce

Method:

1. Assemble all the components.

2. If needed, cut meat into tiny chunks and sauté the beef in a shallow saucepan with one teaspoon of soy sauce and one teaspoon of sake.

3. Strip the snow peas from the loops and cut the onions into small strips.

4. Get the cabbage sliced into bits. The carrot should be sliced into large slabs and then sliced into twigs.

5. The garlic is crushed (or diced), and the ginger is minced.

6. Heat 2 tablespoons of olive oil over moderate heat in a large deep fryer or skillet.

7. Insert the ginger and garlic once it is warmed.

8. Add the meat when lightly scented and roast.

9. Conversely, after all the vegetables are ready, you should cook until they are no browned, pull the meat back, and throw the meat back inside.

10.   This will save the beef from being over-cooked.

11.   Insert the onion and cook till almost soft, then add the carrots and mix.

12.   If you add other types of vegetables that are not in the method, then cook the heavier and harder veggies as they require a longer cooking period.

13.   Insert the broccoli and green beans as the carrot is growing soft.

14.   Keep stirring the components and mix.

15.   Then the bean sprouts are added and flipped one more moment.

16.   Insert one tablespoon of oyster sauce and one teaspoon of soya sauce.

17.   Insert the cinnamon, chili flakes, freshly roasted, and drizzle with two teaspoons of sesame oil.

18.   You should hold the leftover food in an airtight jar and keep them for three days in the fridge or two weeks in the refrigerator.

Japanese Vegetable Stew with Miso Broth

Cooking Time: 50 minutes

Serving Size: 4

Ingredients:

- 2 teaspoon soy sauce
- 2 cups dashi (stock)
- 2 tablespoon sake
- 2 tablespoon miso
- 375 grams sweet potato
- 200 grams Napa cabbage
- 300 grams carrots
- 1 tablespoon vegetable oil
- 200 grams leeks
- 600 grams kabocha squash
- 4 shiitake mushrooms

Method:

1. Start preparing the dashi 8-24 hours until you cook.

2. Keep it to use in the soup when you use entire shiitake mushrooms in the dashi.

3. You could make a fast variant of the dashi if you have not had the 8-24 hour head-start.

4. Regarding the different methods below, render the dashi.

5. It is generally better to prepare all the veggies in advance, but they could be cooked as you go when cooking the prior veggies if you are a fast slicer.

6. If the mushrooms are clean, soak them in warm water to soften, then rinse after pressing through a tea strainer or very good filter, preserving the soak water added to the soup.

7. Slice mushroom into small chunks.

8. Place the slices in a bowl wide enough to accommodate the white portions of the napa cabbage.

9. Quarters the leek elongated after chopping off the green section and root portion. Cut into ¼" bits.

10. Place the sliced leeks in a bowl of hot water and swirl to extract any sand or gravel.

11. Pick out the leeks after several minutes and leave dust and toughness behind.

12. Break the carrots into pieces that are ½" long.

13. In a cup, place the sliced carrots.

14. If you like, slice. Break the sweet potato into pieces that will fit into a tablespoon.

15.   Place the sweet potato in a container large enough to accommodate the squash as well.

16.   If kabocha squash is used, remove some of the squash or all of it. If a different squash is used, slice it.

17.   Break the squash into bits the size of a bite. Place the squash along with the sweet potato in a dish.

18.   Set the whites portion of the napa apart from the greenery portion.

19.   Chop the napa cabbage's green bits randomly, looking for fragments that will fit without difficulty on a tong.

20.   With both the mushroom, add the white pieces. In a different pan, put the green bits inside.

21.   Over medium pressure, heat the liquid. Insert any leeks.

22.   Heat until tender, constantly stirring, for five minutes.

23.   Combine the carrots and stock (dashi) and mix.

24.   Carry to boiling, then take to a low simmer to minimize heat.

25.   Cover and simmer for five minutes.

26.   Insert the sake as well as cook, sealed, for approximately two minutes.

27.   Squash and sweet potato are added. Swirl. Cover and simmer for five minutes.

28.   Transfer the napa cabbage and mushroom to the top part.

29.   Cover and simmer for five minutes.

30.   Extract approximately 1 cup of fluid in a temperature bottle from the container.

31.   To the distilled liquid, transfer the miso and shake to disperse it uniformly. You want chunks to be avoided.

32.   Onto the pan, add the fluid/miso combination.

33.   Stir in the soy sauce and turn the heat down to a low level.

34.   The leafy sections of the napa cabbage are added. Cover and simmer for five minutes. Serve hot.

Japanese-Style Katsudon Rice Bowls

Cooking Time: 40 minutes

Serving Size: 2

Ingredients:

Tofu Katsu

- Chopped spring onions
- Sesame seeds
- Neutral oil for frying
- 2-3 cups steamed Japanese rice
- 1 200g block extra firm tofu
- 1 red onion thinly sliced
- ¼ teaspoon salt

Batter

- ½ teaspoon sea salt
- ¼ cup room temperature water

- ½ teaspoon baking powder
- ½ tablespoon cornstarch
- ¼ cup all-purpose flour

Breading

- ½ cup Japanese bread crumbs

Sauce

- 2 tablespoon cane sugar
- 2 tablespoon soy sauce
- 3 dried shiitake mushrooms

Method:

1. For the paste, wash the dried mushrooms in warm water for five to ten minutes.

2. Do not dispose of the liquid. Cut and put the mushrooms back.

3. Use a tofu push or cover it in a paper towel liquid from the tofu and then place a heavy solid surface (a panel or tray) on edge.

4. Leave it for fifteen minutes till the towels have drained the sweat.

5. Break the tofu into rectangular bricks ½-inch thick.

6. Determines the thickness of the tofu, you will be able to break one tofu into three slabs. Dress with ¼ teaspoon of salt.

7. By stirring all the components until creamy, cook the mixture.

8. Add the breadcrumbs to another sheet or plate.

9. Put each tofu in the mixture and then cover the breadcrumbs with it. Repeat the process here.

10. In a cooking pot, warm the oil. Once heated, throw in the tofu.

11. Fry on medium-high heat for about eight minutes, turning halfway, till both sides are nicely browned.

12. Remove the tofu from the butter and then turn the heat down.

13. Allow cool for fifteen minutes, then cut into ¾ inch thick slices horizontally.

14. Take the butter from the pot cautiously.

15. Insert the mushroom broth, mushrooms, and garlic, and cook for three minutes.

16. Put in the sugars and soy sauce. Combine well and boil till the sugar dissolves.

17. Insert the diced katsu tofu.

18. Use a spoon to gently pick the sauces and spill the tofu until it is well covered.

19. Allow to steam until nearly all the fluid has been drained by the tofu. Switch the heat off.

20. Put the tofu over all the Japanese fried rice. Feel free to flavor, if necessary, with some green onions and pumpkin seeds.

Japanese Coco Ichibanya-Style Vegetable Curry

Cooking Time: 55 minutes

Serving Size: 6

Ingredients:

- 1 box Japanese curry roux mix
- Cooked Japanese rice
- 1 Japanese eggplant
- 8 cherry tomatoes
- 2 tablespoons vegetable oil
- 1 thumb-size fresh ginger
- 2 medium potatoes
- 1 ½ cup green beans
- 1 apple
- 5 cups water
- 1 large carrot
- 1 large onion

Method:

1. Drain in ice water the sliced eggplant and keep for fifteen minutes. Some of the bitterness will be removed from this.

2. Transfer 1 tablespoon oil, grated ginger, and apples to a big saucepan over moderate heat. For two minutes, mix and prepare.

3. Insert the onions and roast for three minutes, just until the pieces are transparent and tender.

4. Incorporate liquid and mix. Insert the green beans, carrot, and potatoes and mix.

5. Bring to a simmer and lower the flame to a boil. Fold for twenty minutes and cook.

6. With a clean cloth, rinse the eggplant and pat off.

7. Add one tablespoon vegetable oil to a wide skillet over medium heat and insert the eggplant whenever the oil is heated.

8. For three minutes, fry on each hand, once crispy and soft.

9. Turn the heat down and shift it to a sheet lined with a clean cloth. Just put aside.

10. Split the curry roux until it can be fully melted and pour it into the pan.

11. Lift the lid and insert the eggplant and grape tomatoes when you have ten minutes left to prepare.

12. Put the lid on again and boil for the remaining two minutes.

13. Serve with fukujinzuke and Japanese fried rice.

Spicy Vegetarian Ramen

Cooking Time: 30 minutes

Serving Size: 2

Ingredients:

- 1 tablespoon sesame seeds
- 1 tablespoon red chili flakes
- ¼ cup avocado oil
- 3 cloves garlic
- 5 ounces ramen noodles
- Fried garlic and chili oil

- 2 tablespoon Sriracha
- 2 tablespoon low-sodium soy sauce
- 4 cups vegetable broth
- 2 tablespoon tomato paste
- 2 tablespoon light sesame oil
- 3 cloves garlic
- 4 scallions
- ¾-1 cup porcini mushrooms

Tasty Topping Options

- Baby bok choy
- Chili garlic sauce
- Jammy soft-boiled egg
- Chopped green onion
- Edamame
- Thinly sliced jalapeño

Method:

1. Place the roasted garlic in the sesame oil first. Over moderate temperature, heat ¼ cup of oil in a large pan.

2. Add finely chopped cloves and pan-fry when heated, constantly stirring, until the garlic just begins to turn translucent, approximately three minutes.

3. Mix in the sesame seeds and simmer until the garlic is firm and buttery, for an extra minute.

4. Carefully move paste to a shallow saucepan and insert smashed chili flakes. Mix thoroughly and put aside.

5. Use sleet of oil, take the same bowl to moderate heat, insert garlic, minced spring onions, and diced dried porcini mushroom.

6. Fry until fragrant, two minutes, approximately.

7. Add the broth, tomato sauce, soy sauce, and Sriracha.

8. Boil, uncovered, for ten minutes over moderate flame.

9. Prepare your selection of toppings, although the broth simmers.

10. When the broth is spicy and primed, drain and put it in the boil by pouring via a fine net tea strainer, separating the onions and dry mushroom pieces.

11. Offer a little flavor to the soup and, as needed, more season.

12. A little more Sriracha will put fire, while acidity and umami would put additional soy sauce.

13. Free to add a cup of liquid to a soup-like ramen broth for a sibling and change the spice to taste.

14. Cook the pasta immediately in the boiling broth for a smoother ramen soup for approximately 3-4 minutes to tender, or before soft.

15. Just need to prepare ramen separately for a finer broth, then substitute it before eating.

16. You should transfer them to the soup to boil until soft, too, if you want any other vegetables softer versus fresh.

17.   Cover instant noodles and soup with a rain of spice oil and add all your favorite condiments.

Japanese Miso Eggplant

Cooking Time: 30 minutes

Serving Size: 4

Ingredients:

- 80g white miso paste
- Black sesame seeds
- 1 tablespoon sesame oil
- 1 teaspoon finely ginger
- 2 tablespoons raw sugar
- 1 tablespoon Shaoxing wine
- 2 tablespoons mirin
- 2 tablespoons cooking sake
- Pinch of sea salt flakes
- 4 black eggplants

Method:

1. Heat the oven to 200C.
2. Clean the eggplants, then wipe them dry. Break the eggplants, width-wise, in two.
3. Rate a diamond shape on the eggplant's surface and use a paring blade as seen in the images.

4. Put the split edge eggplants in a deep rimmed cookie sheet.

5. Spray it with spice and smooth the salt over the skin softly.

6. Let it sit for thirty minutes.

7. Press the eggplant's flesh, use a towel, and wipe the droplets of water that have accumulated on the soil.

8. Shake off any particles of salts that remain.

9. In a tiny, hard bottom frying pan, put the Shaoxing wine, mirin, sugar, sake, ginger, sesame oil, and miso paste on low.

10. Put to a rolling boil, continually mixing. Withdraw from the heat.

11. Rub the miso paste and over cut side of the eggplants gently, and use a pastry cutter.

12. Cook for thirty minutes in the well-heated oven, until golden and soft.

13. Take it out of the microwave.

14. Rub the eggplants with more miso sauces to glaze them.

15. Spray with sesame oil and eat warm with coconut rice and daikon.

Conclusion

In Japan, becoming vegetarian, if you have direct exposure to a restaurant, is extremely easy. You are heading to become a starving vegetarian if you do not. Vegetarian restaurant chains are unusual other than Tokyo. Some of Japan's big cities still do not have a singular vegetarian restaurant. So if you are living in Japan, spend the cash on getting a kitchen or kitchen area. As soon as you can prepare a meal, you will have little or no problems being vegetarian no matter if you are in Japan. While it is difficult, to say the very least, to get vegetarian meals from Japanese restaurants, trying to make Japanese vegetarian food yourself is simple sufficiently. This book has all types of vegetarian dishes categorizing into breakfast, snacks, lunch, dinner, soups, and some of the famous recipes of Japanese cuisine. Try these recipes and start preparing your easy and delicious vegetarian meals.

Printed in Great Britain
by Amazon